Advanced Pa[per]
Airplanes For Kids
And Adults

Extra Templates

Andrew R Thorne

ISBN: 1544829256
ISBN-13: 978-1544829258

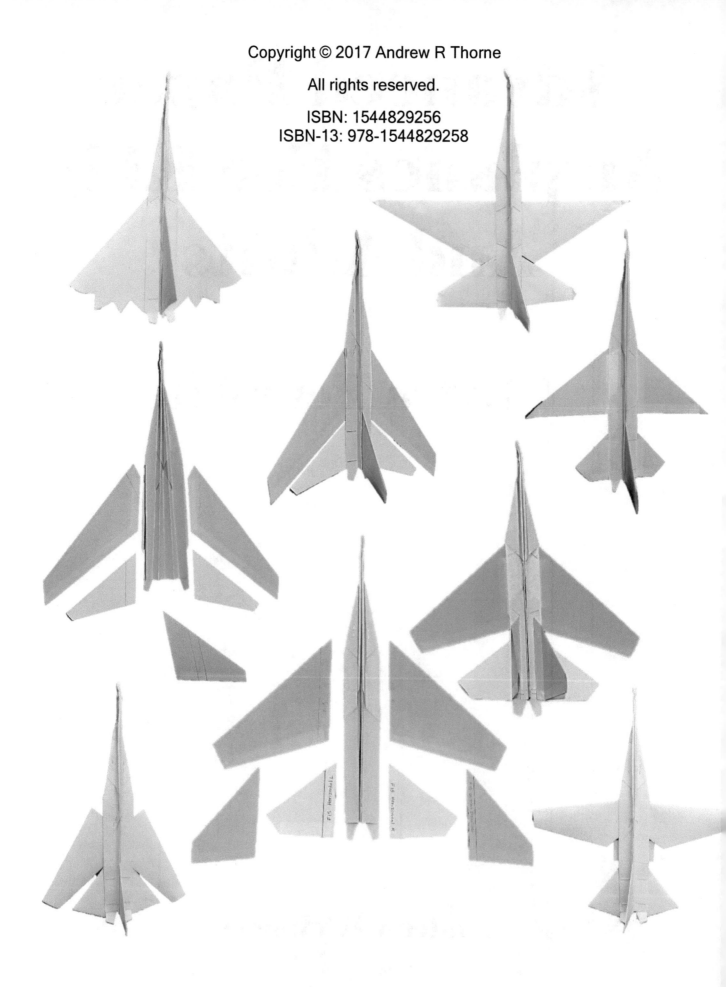

CONTENTS

TEMPLATES

1-1: DELTA WING TEMPLATES:

5-2 Wing

Leading Edge

Trailing Edge

Leading Edge

Trailing Edge

5-2 Vertical Tail

5-3 Vertical Tail

Trailing Edge

Leading Edge

Leading Edge

Trailing Edge

5-3 Vertical Tail

5-2 Wing

Leading Edge

Trailing Edge

Trailing Edge

Leading Edge

5-2 Vertical Tail

5-3 Vertical Tail

Trailing Edge

Leading Edge

Leading Edge

Trailing Edge

5-3 Vertical Tail

5-2 Wing

Leading Edge

Trailing Edge

Leading Edge

Trailing Edge

5-2 Vertical Tail

5-3 Vertical Tail

Trailing Edge

Leading Edge

Leading Edge

Trailing Edge

5-3 Vertical Tail

5-2 Wing

Leading Edge

Trailing Edge

Trailing Edge

Leading Edge

5-2 Vertical Tail

5-3 Vertical Tail

Trailing Edge

Leading Edge

Leading Edge

Trailing Edge

5-3 Vertical Tail

5-2 Wing

Leading Edge

Trailing Edge

Leading Edge

Trailing Edge

5-2 Vertical Tail

5-3 Vertical Tail

Trailing Edge

Leading Edge

Leading Edge

Trailing Edge

5-3 Vertical Tail

5V-1 Wing & Vertical Tail

Leading Edge

Leading Edge

Trailing Edge

Trailing Edge

5V-1 Wing & Vertical Tail

Leading Edge

Trailing Edge

Leading Edge

Trailing Edge

5V-1 Wing & Vertical Tail

Leading Edge

Trailing Edge

Leading Edge

Trailing Edge

5V-1 Wing & Vertical Tail

Leading Edge

Trailing Edge

Leading Edge

Trailing Edge

5V-1 Wing & Vertical Tail

Leading Edge

Trailing Edge

Leading Edge

Trailing Edge

1-2: FIGHTER TEMPLATES:

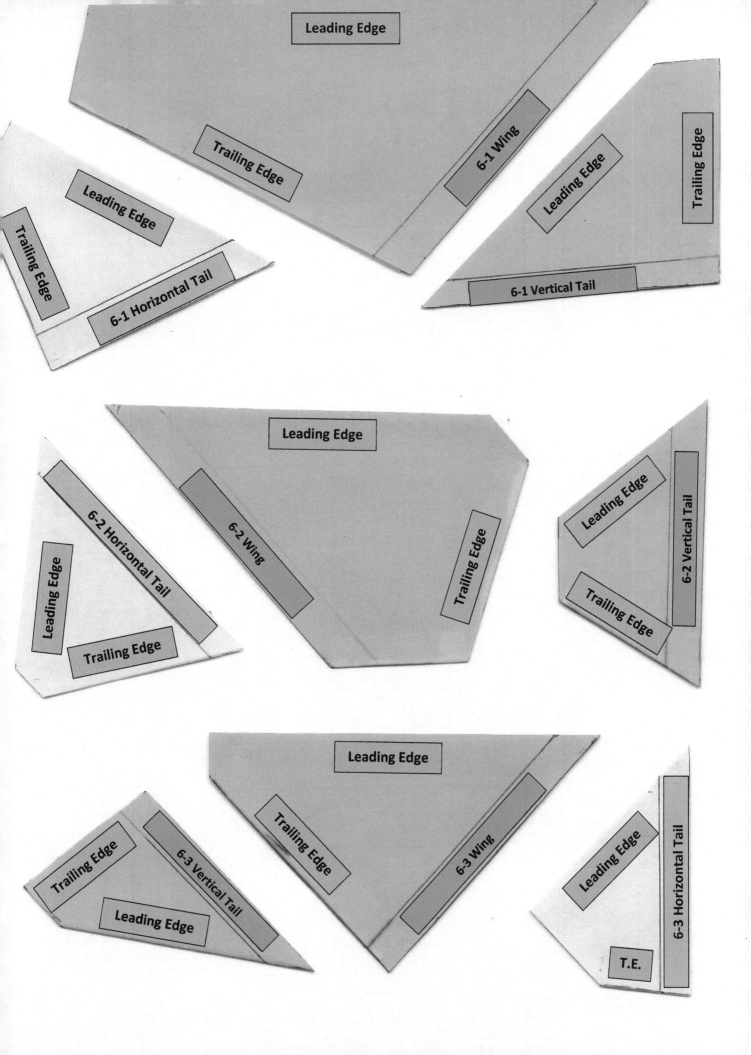

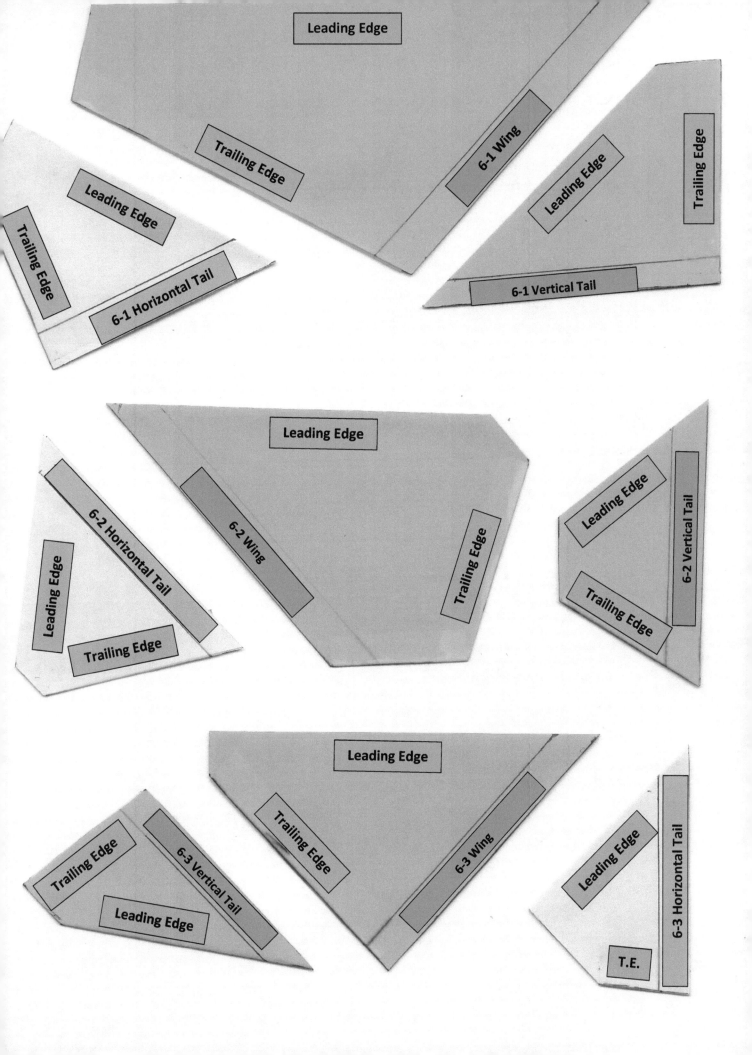

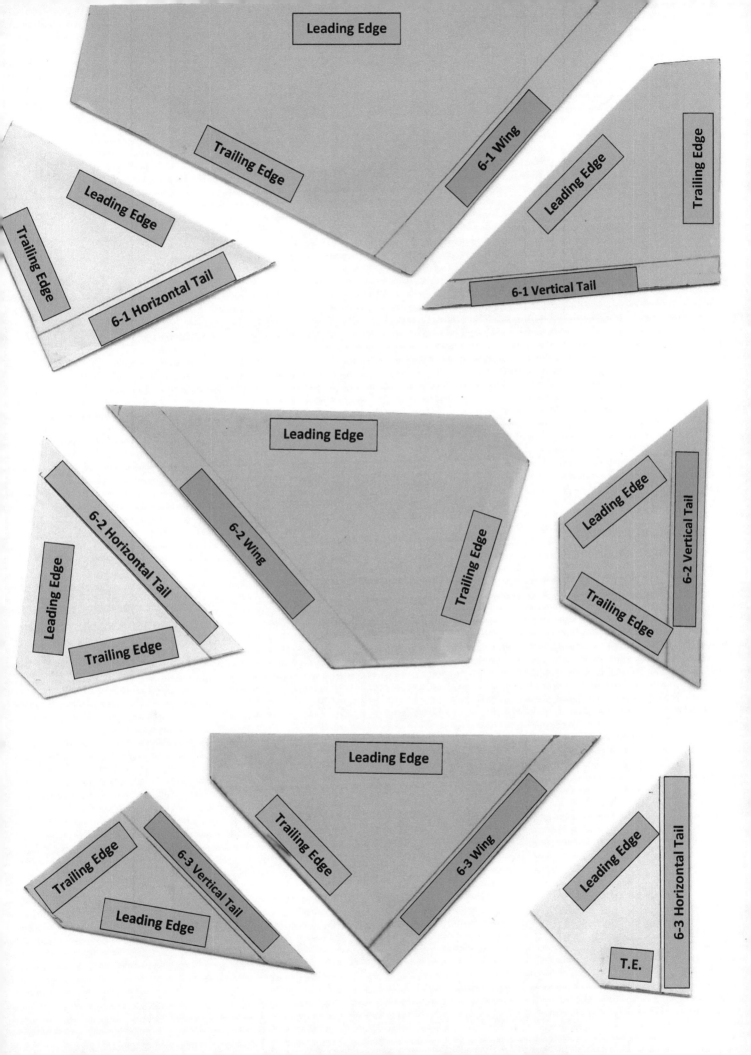

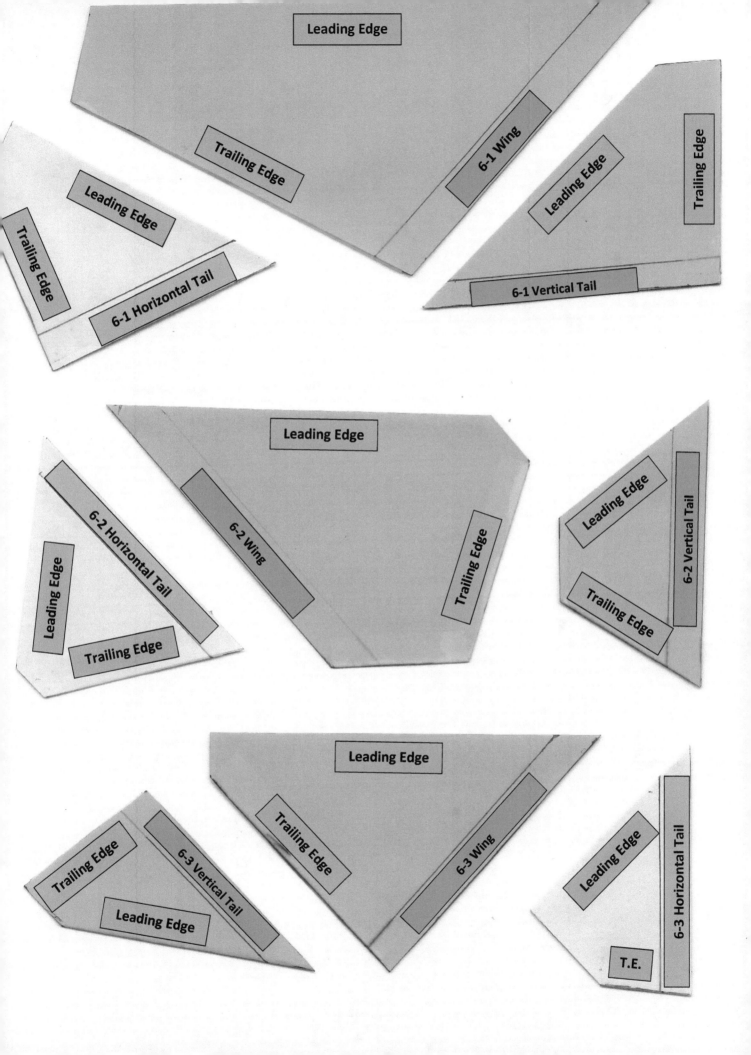

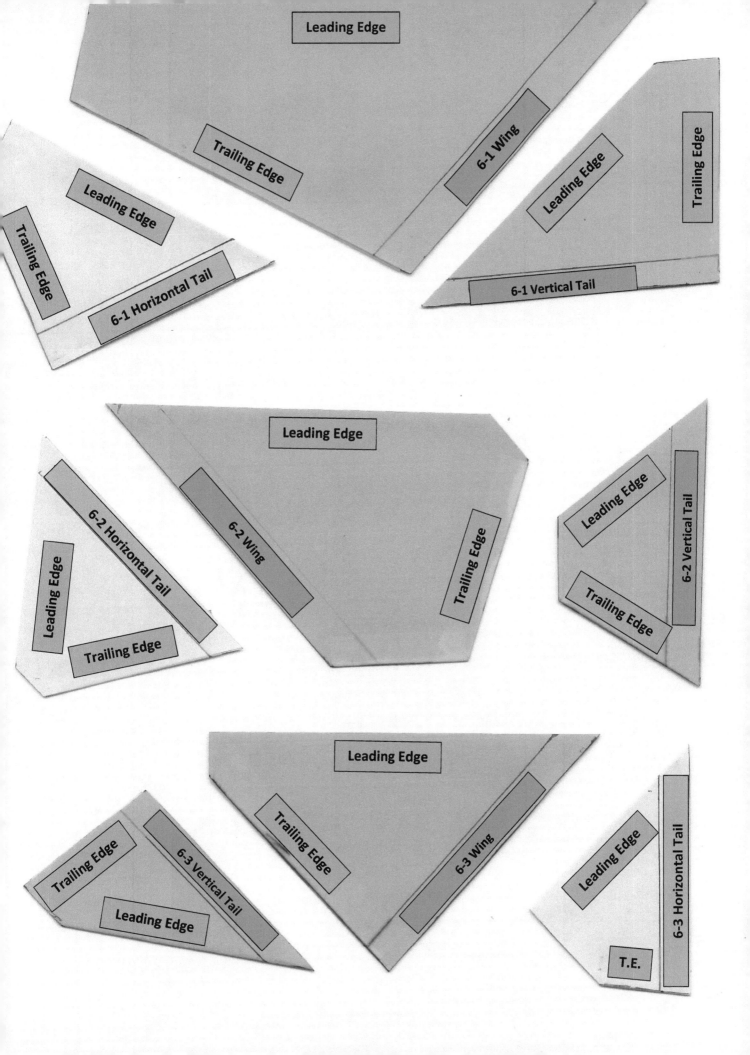

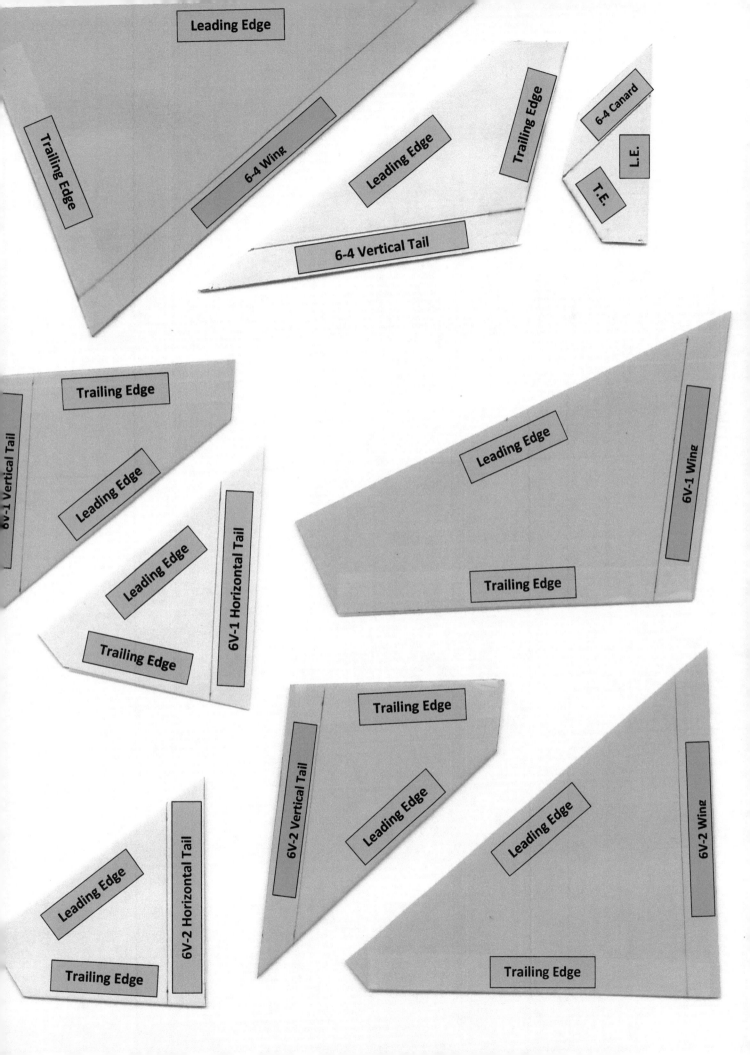

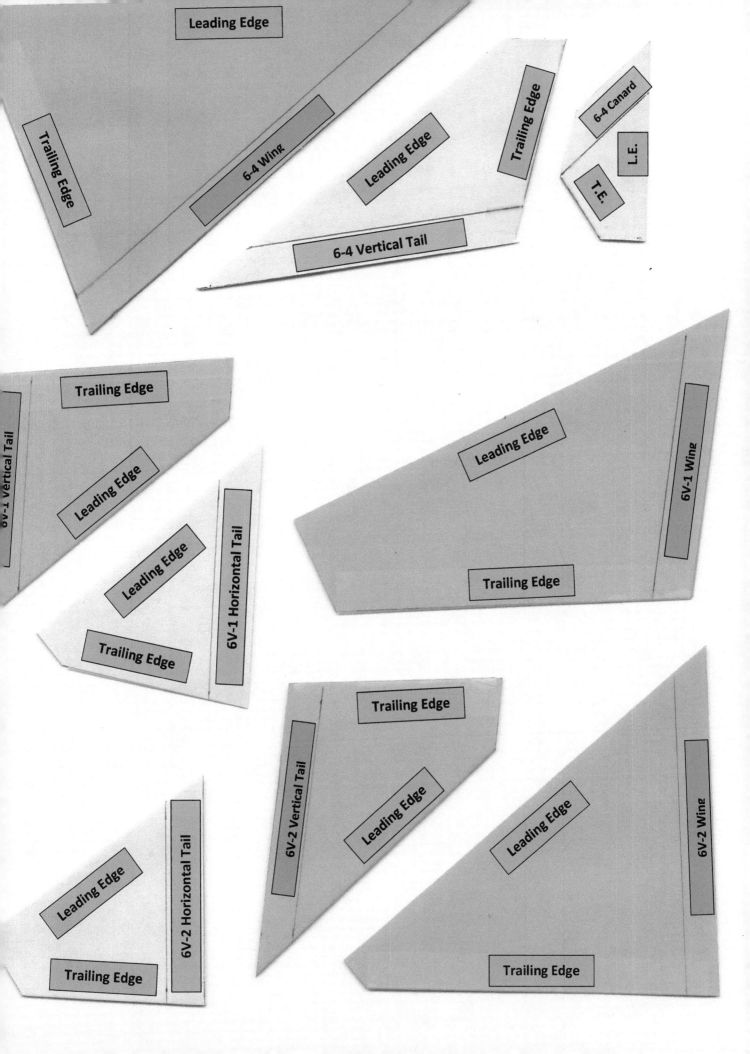

38

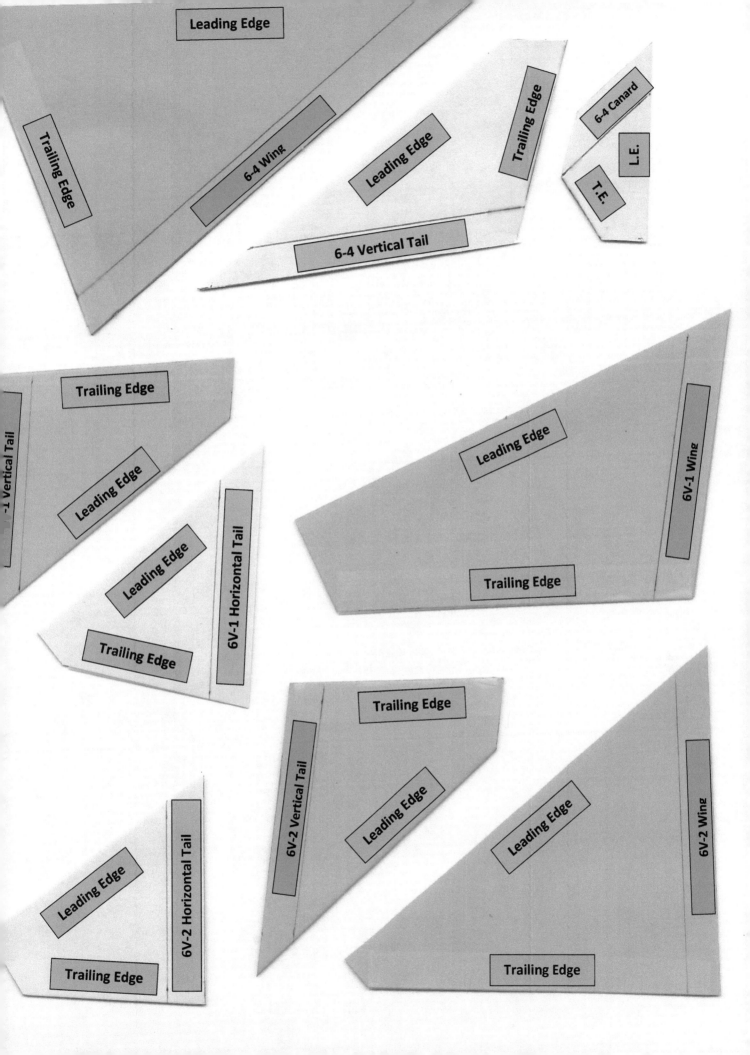

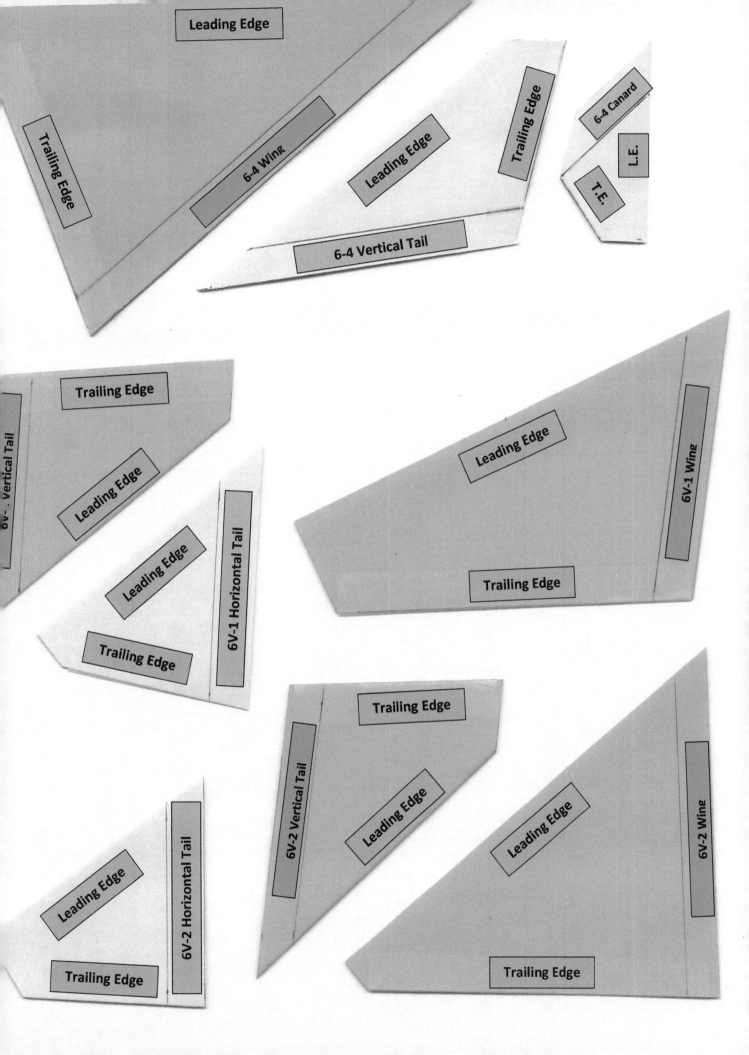

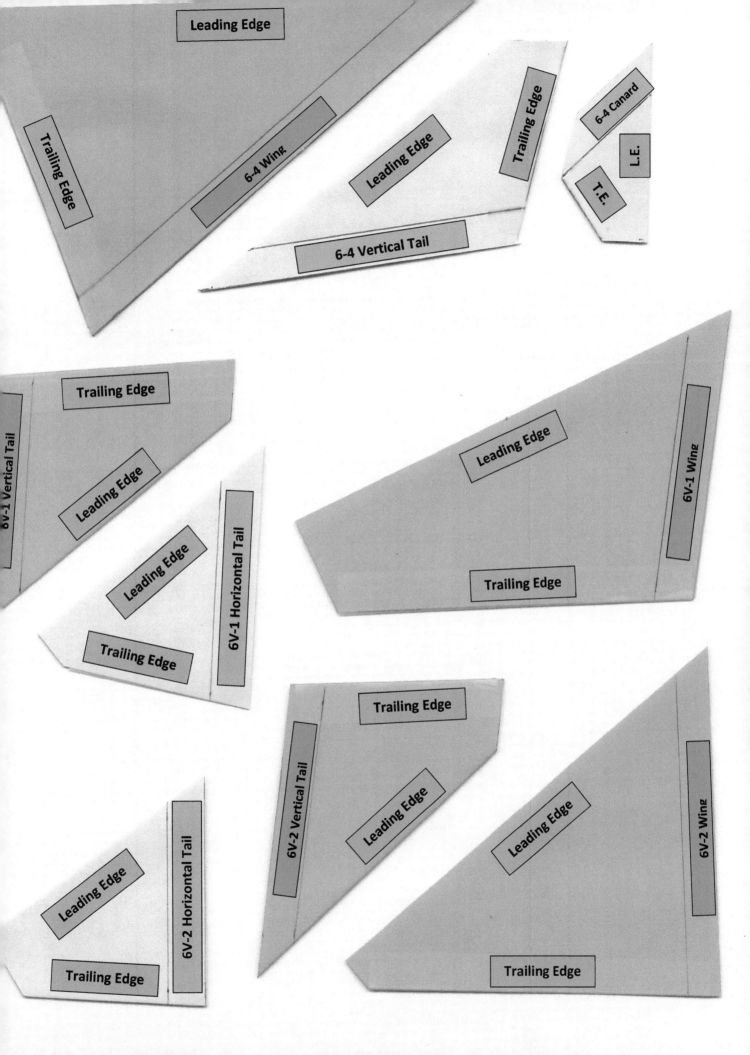

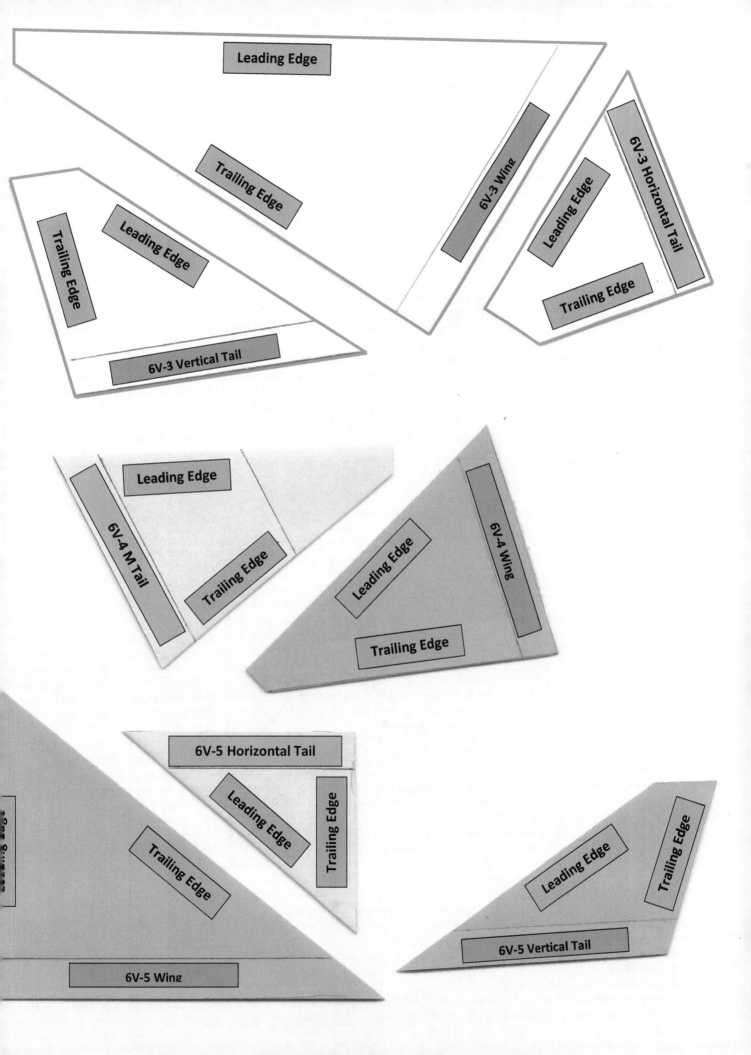

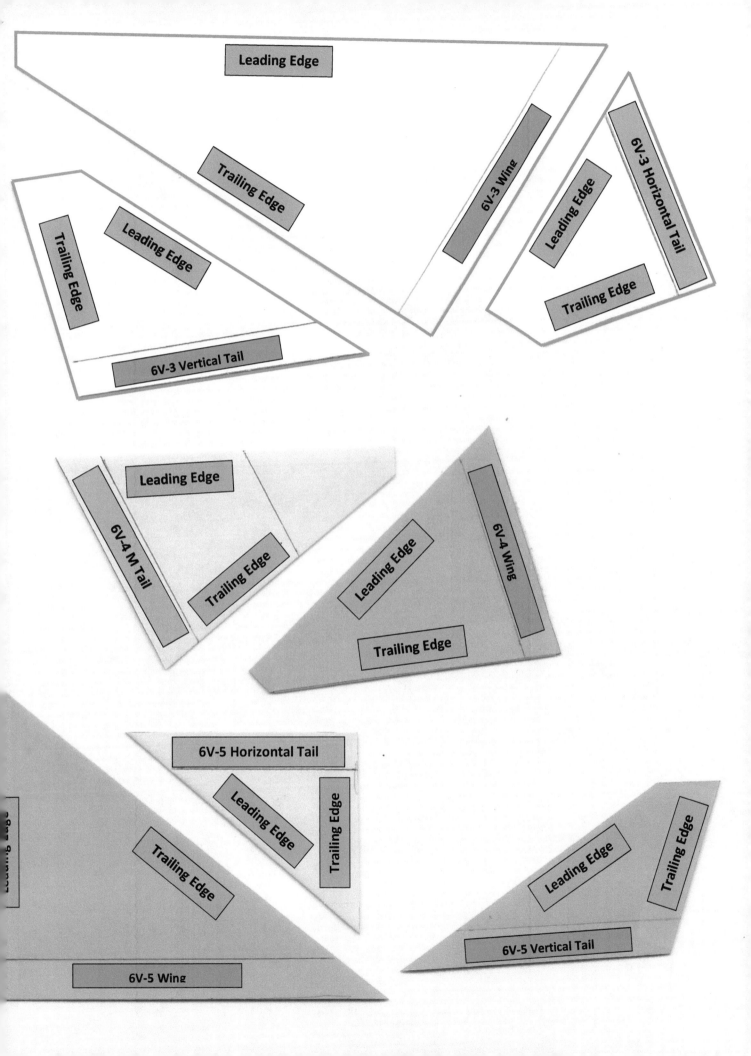

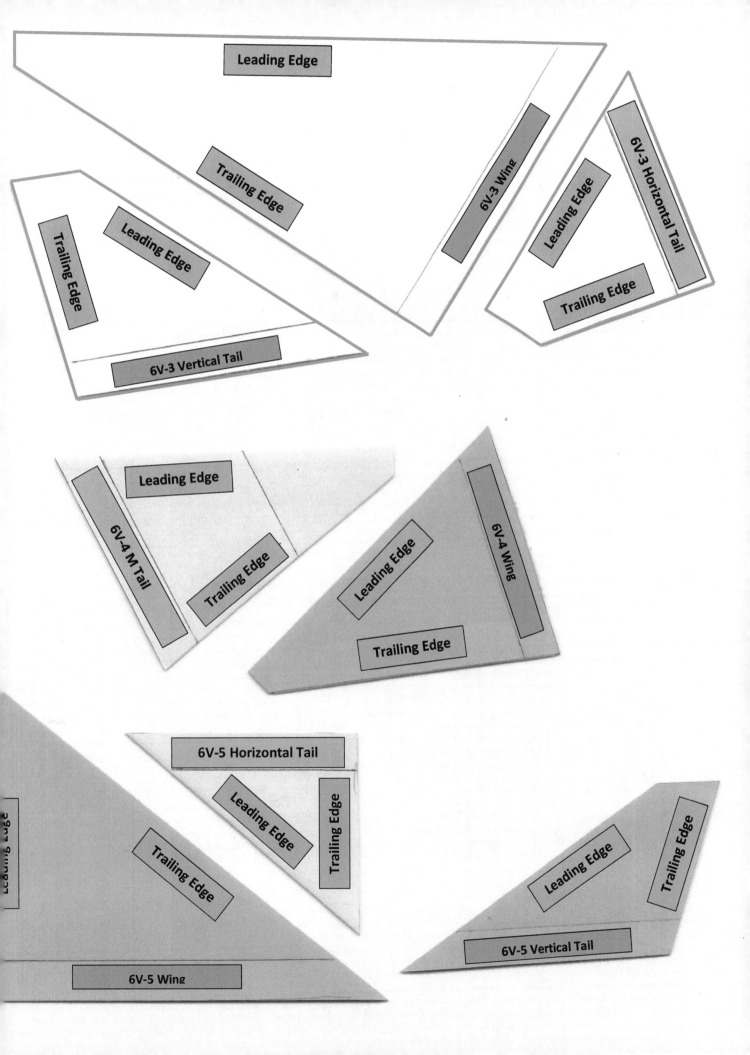

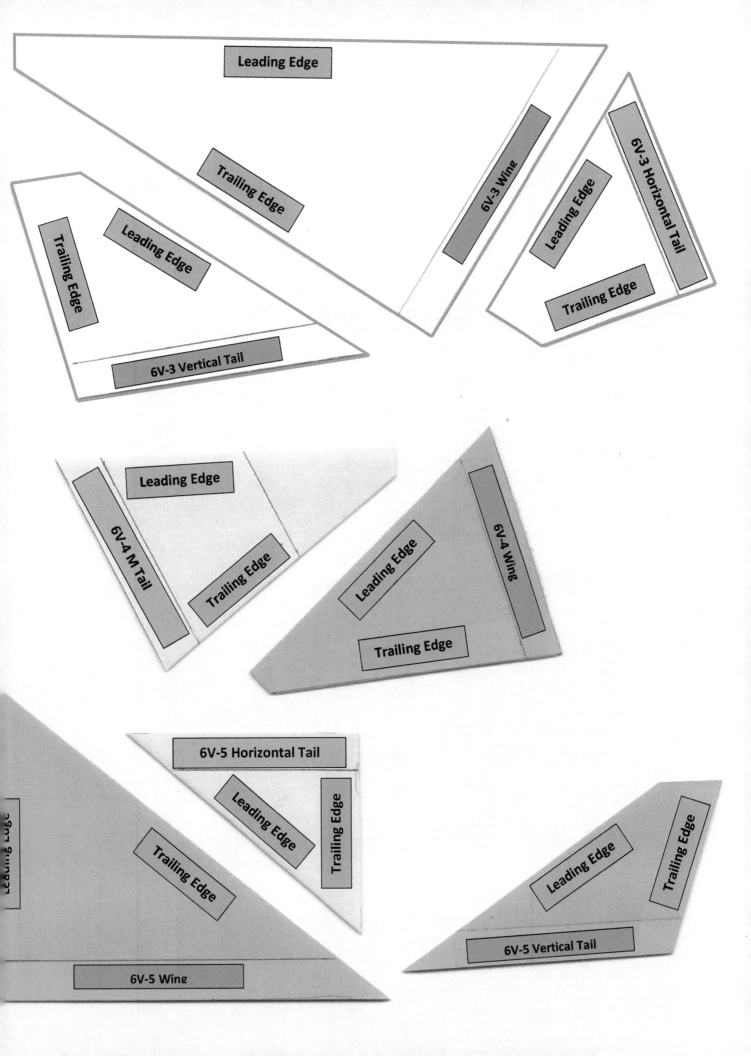

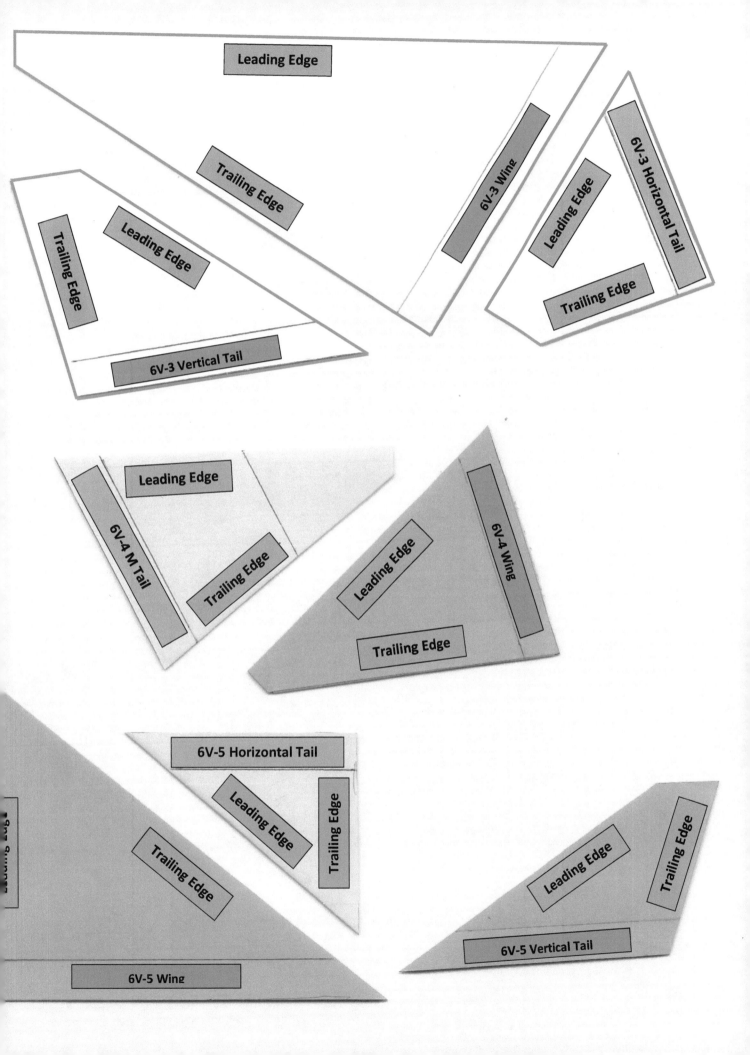

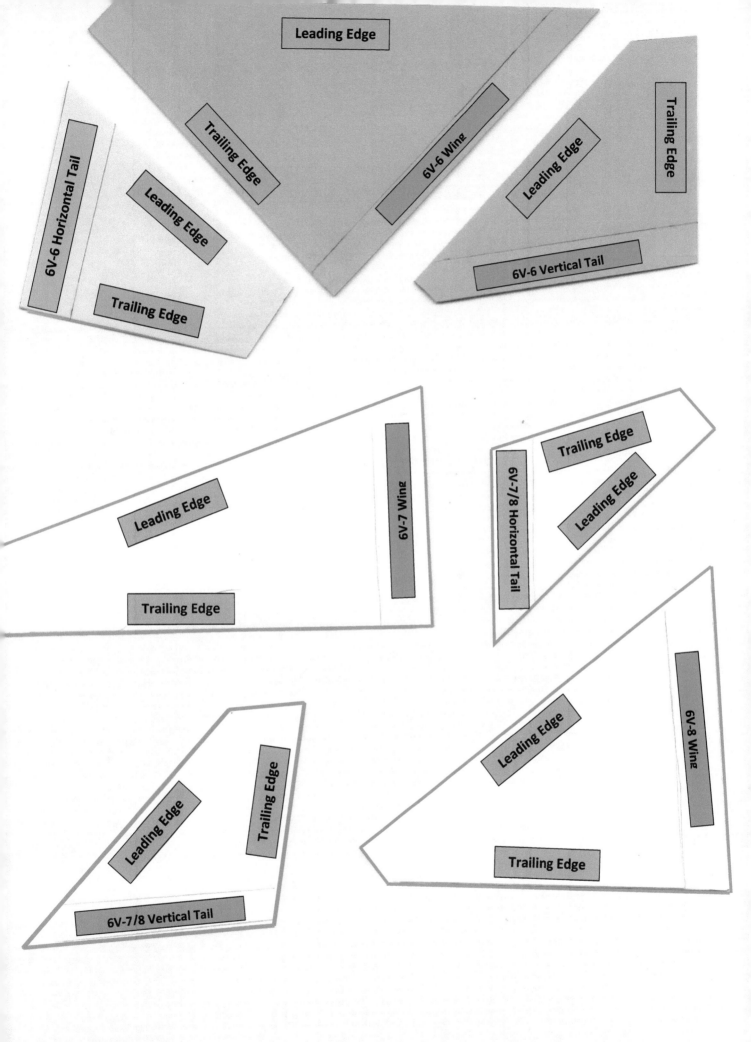

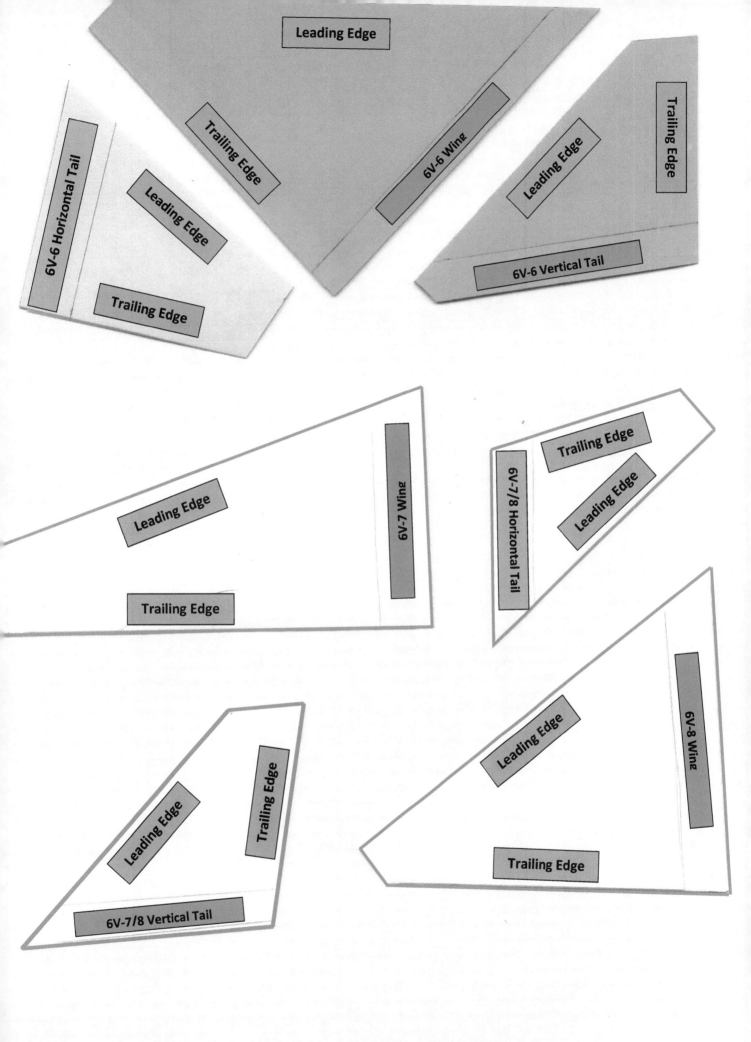

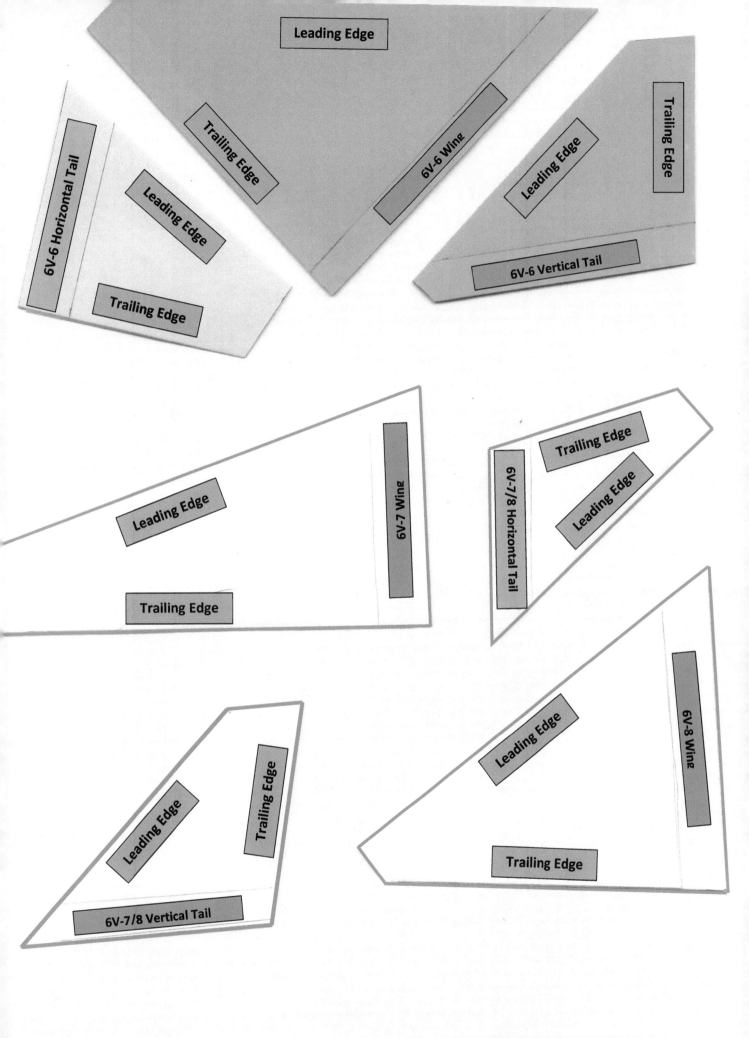

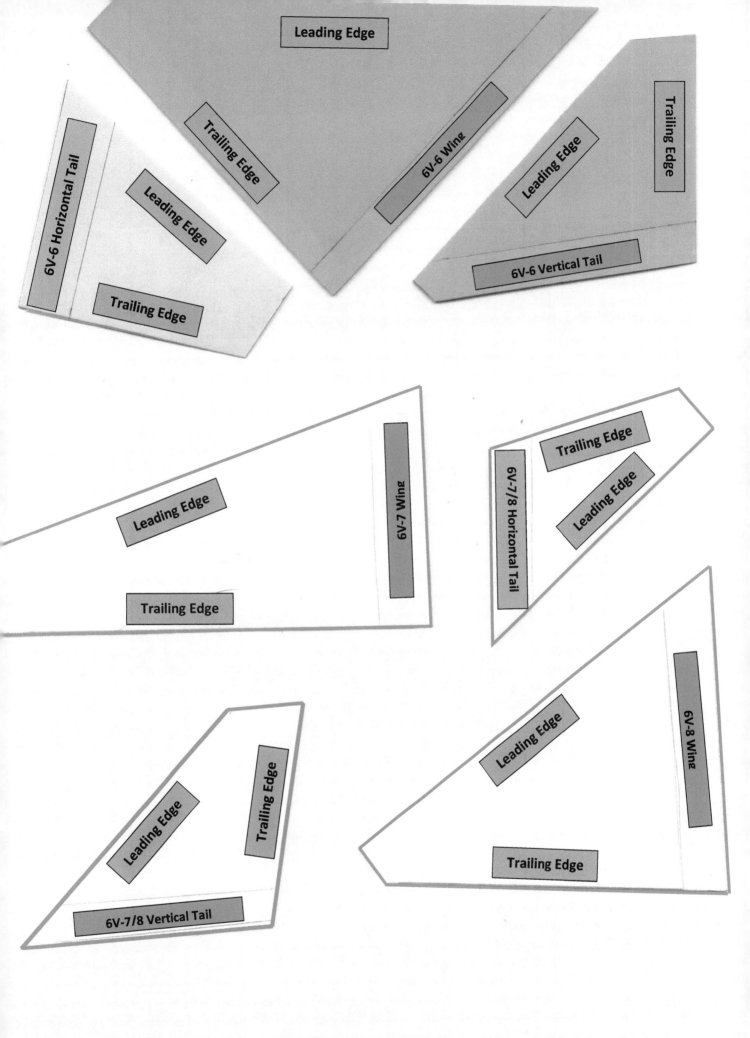

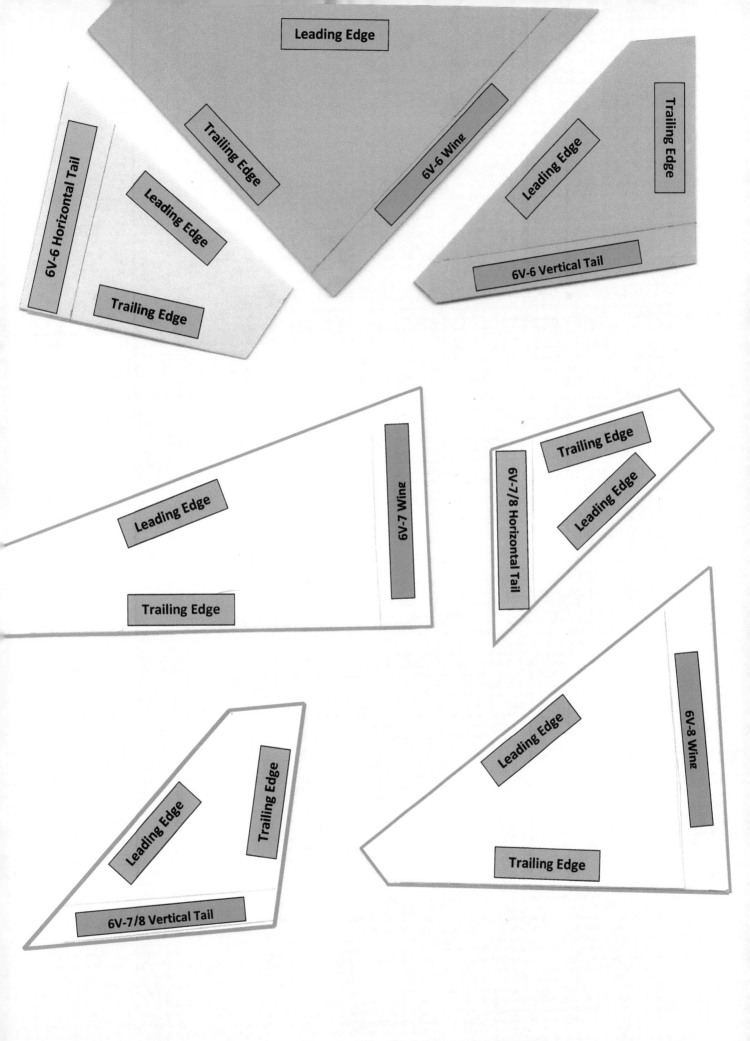

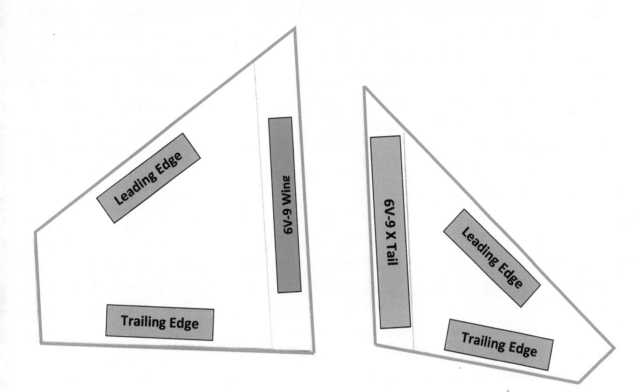

Leading Edge

6V-9 Wing

Trailing Edge

6V-9 X Tail

Leading Edge

Trailing Edge

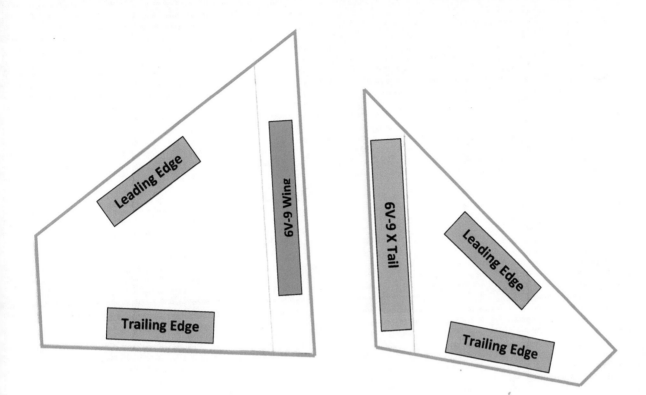

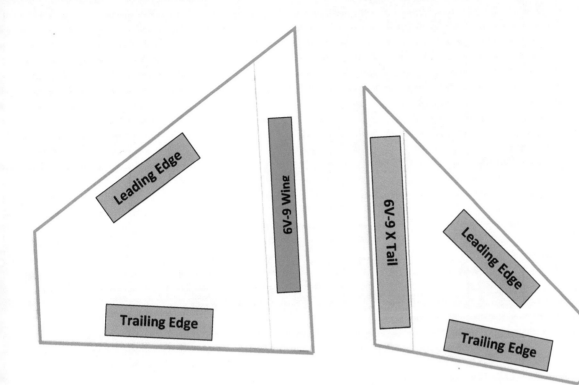

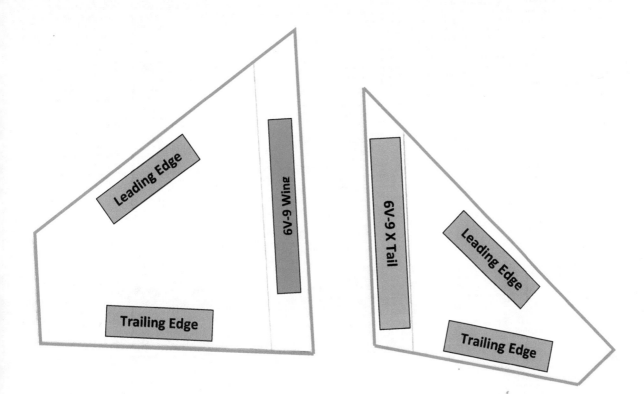

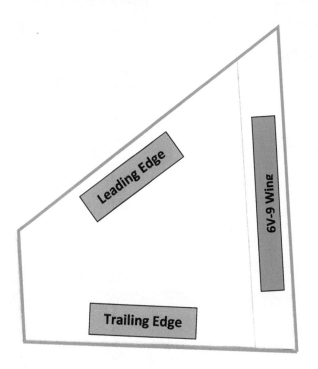

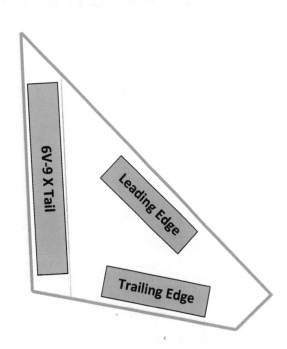

1-3 HIGH ASPECT RATIO TEMPLATES:

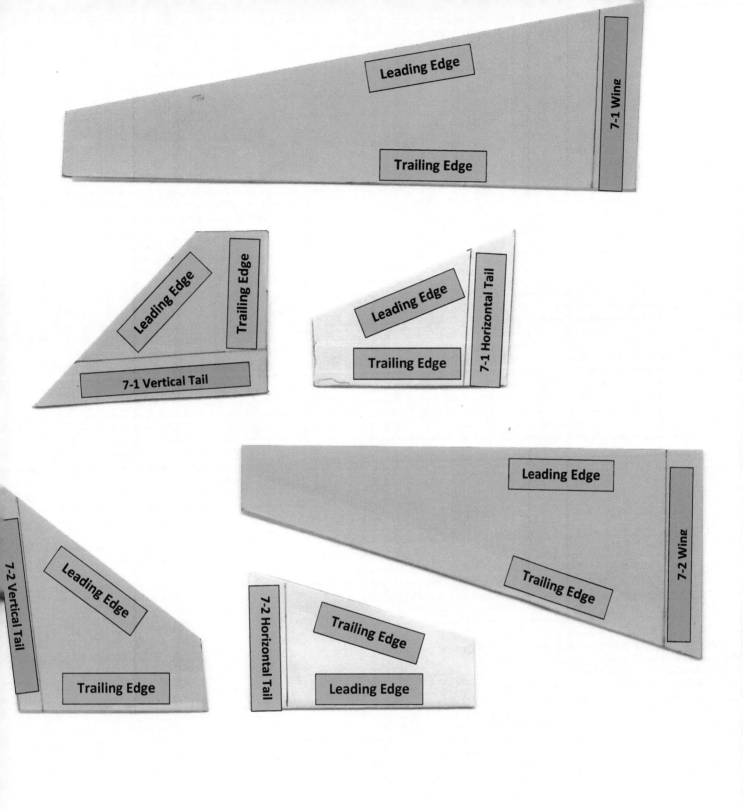

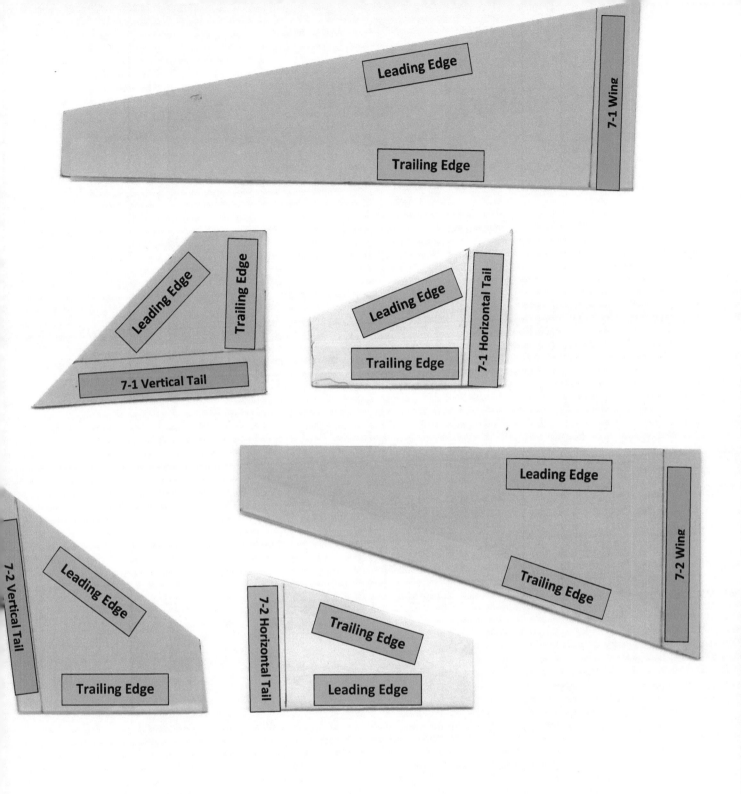

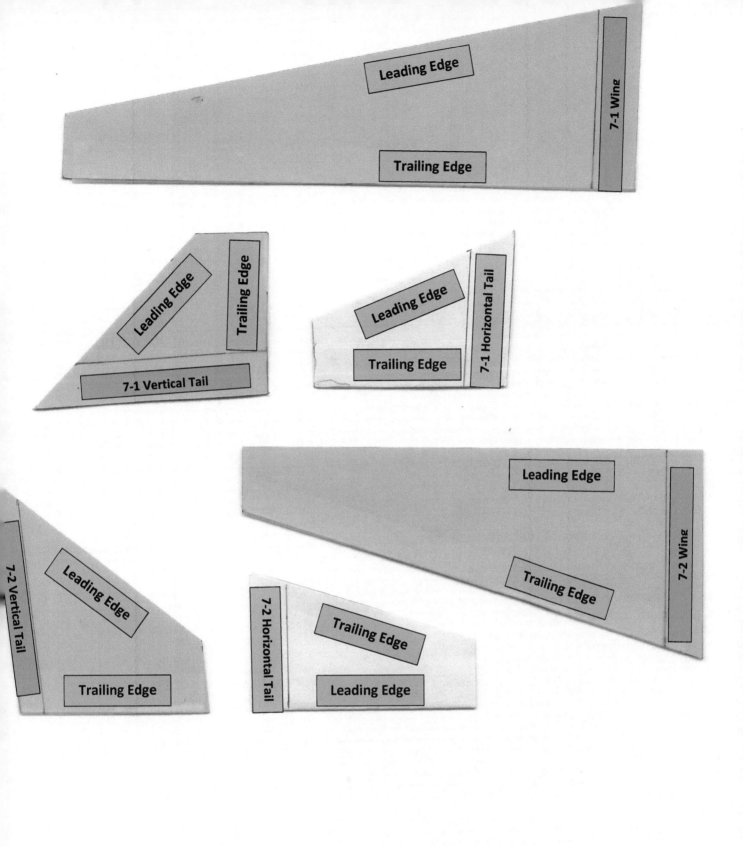

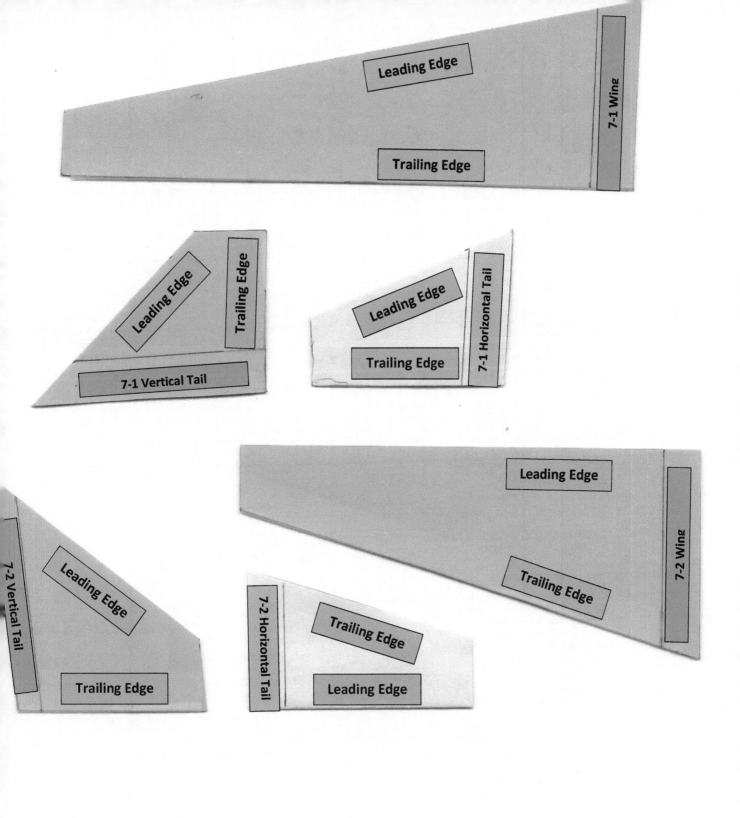

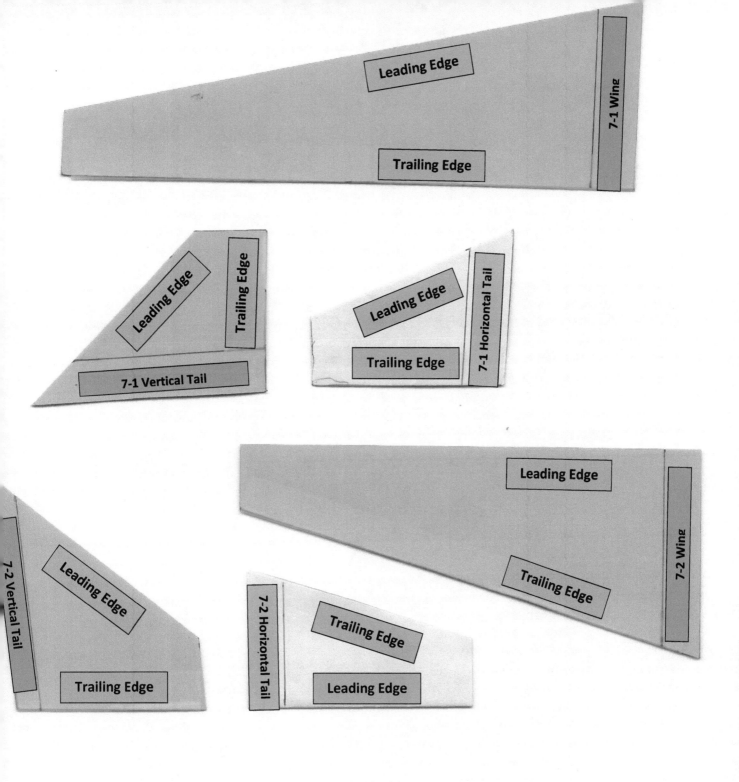

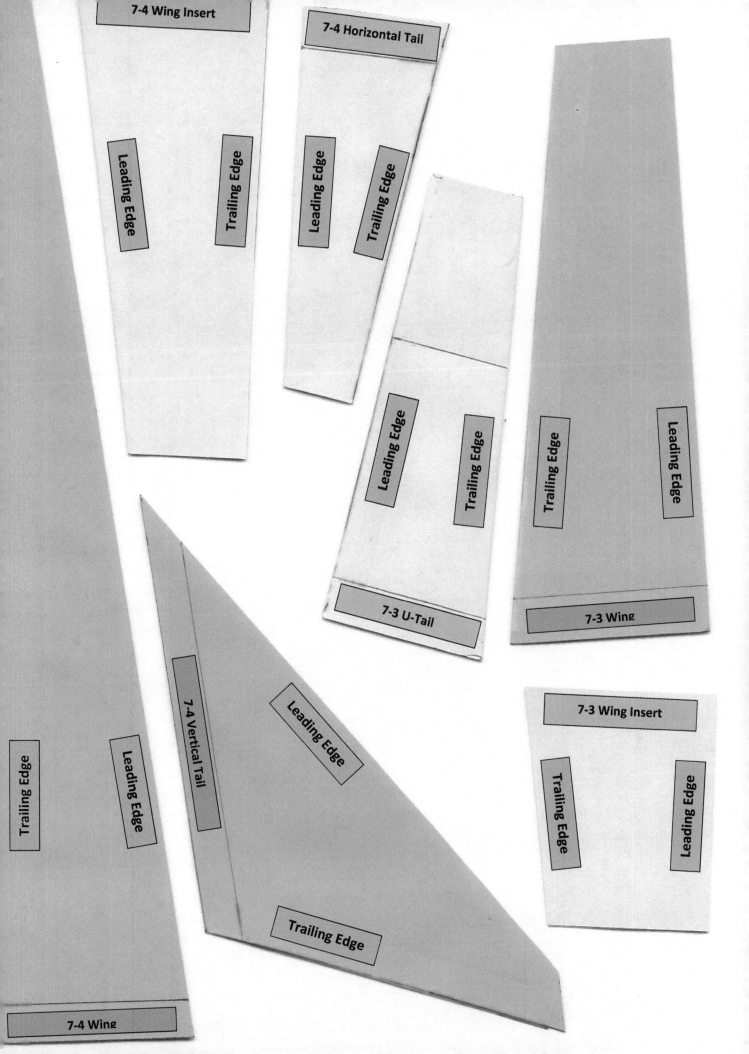

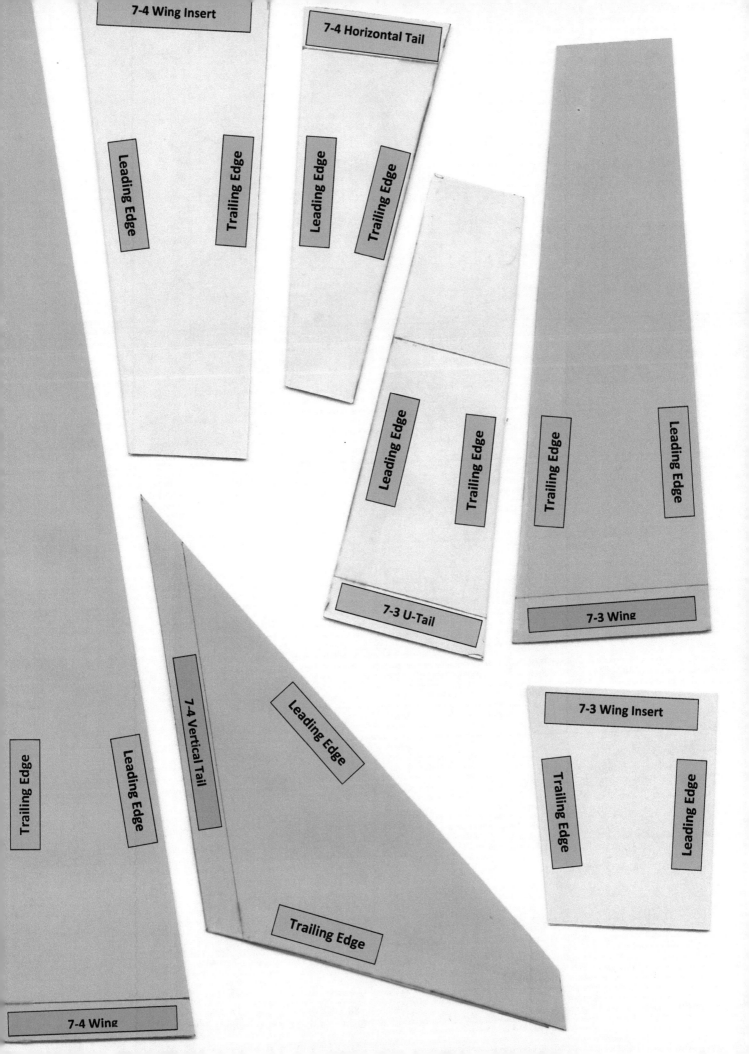

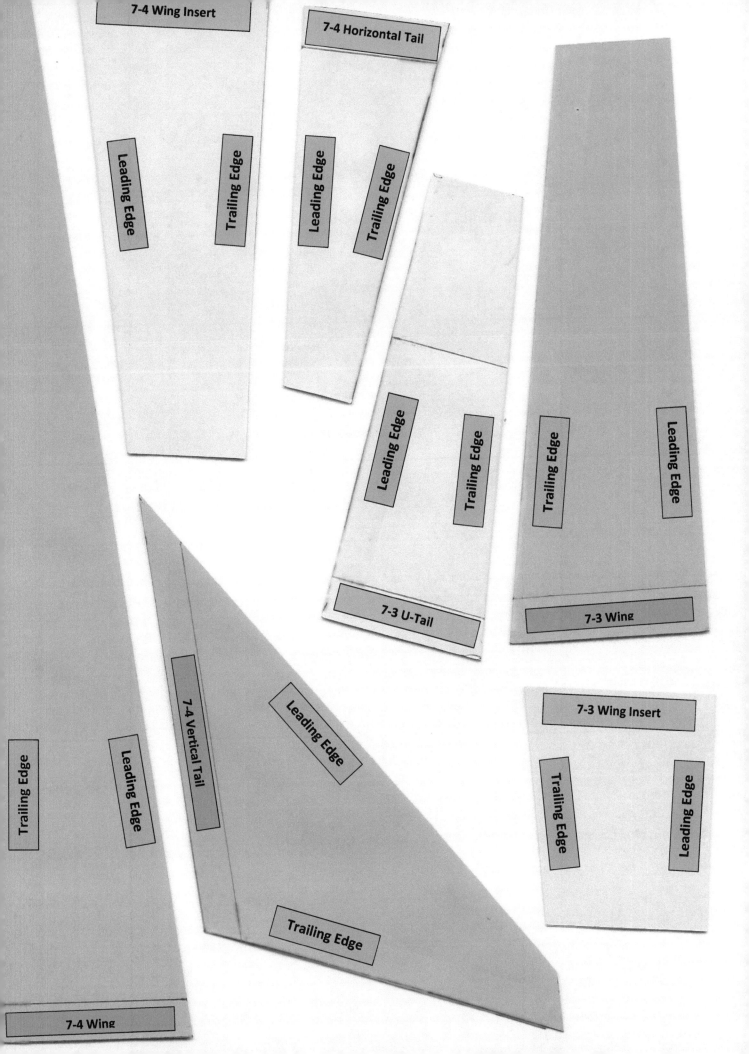

7-4 Wing Insert

Leading Edge

Trailing Edge

7-4 Horizontal Tail

Leading Edge

Trailing Edge

Leading Edge

Trailing Edge

Trailing Edge

Leading Edge

7-3 U-Tail

7-3 Wing

Trailing Edge

Leading Edge

7-4 Vertical Tail

Leading Edge

Trailing Edge

7-3 Wing Insert

Trailing Edge

Leading Edge

7-4 Wing

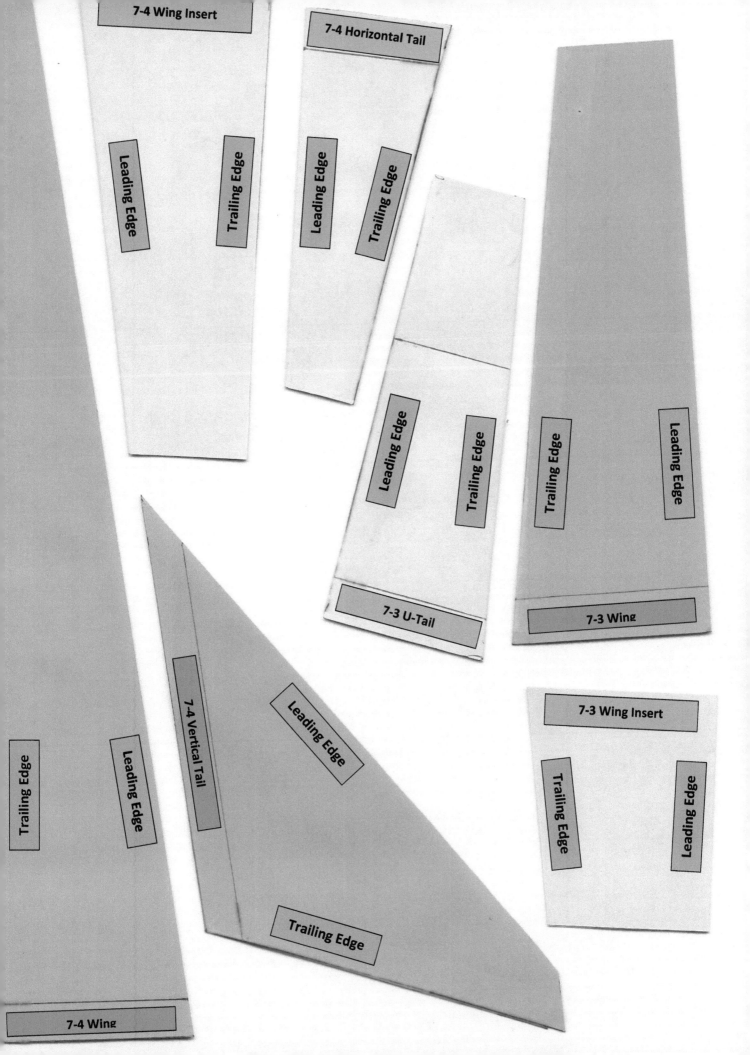

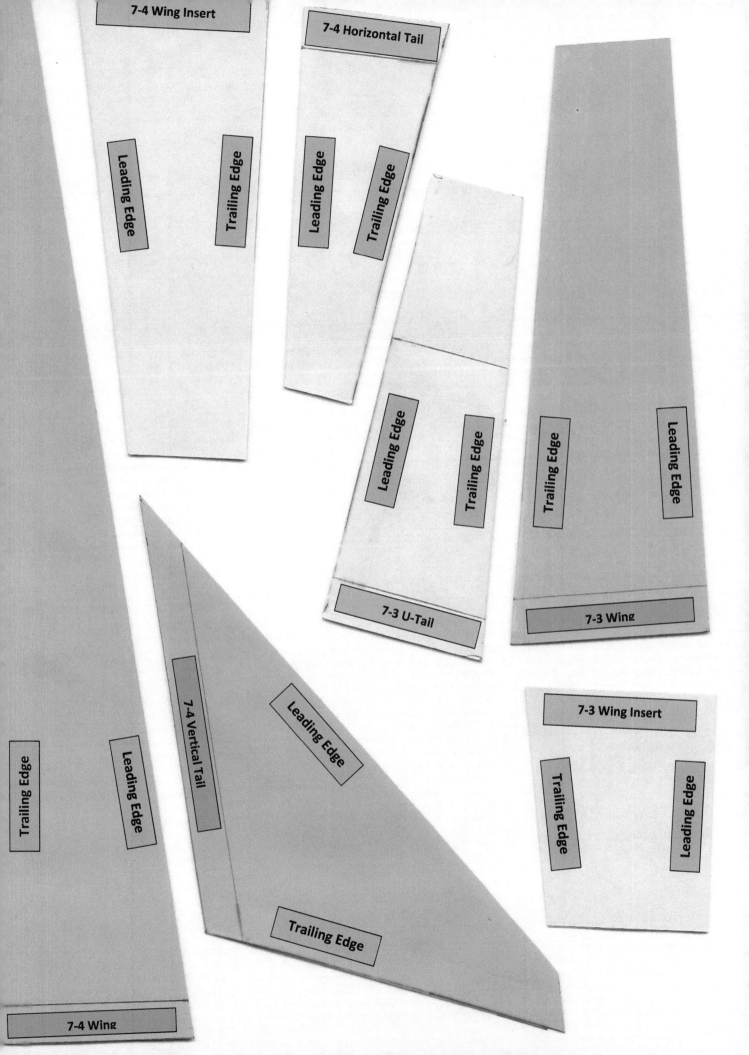

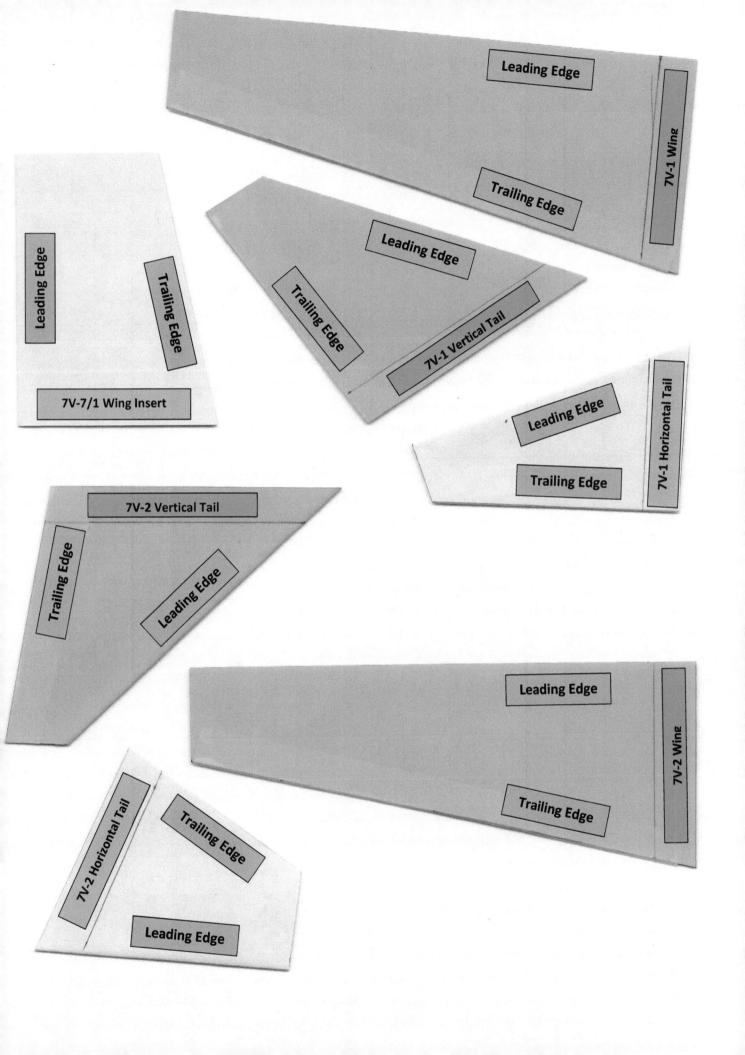

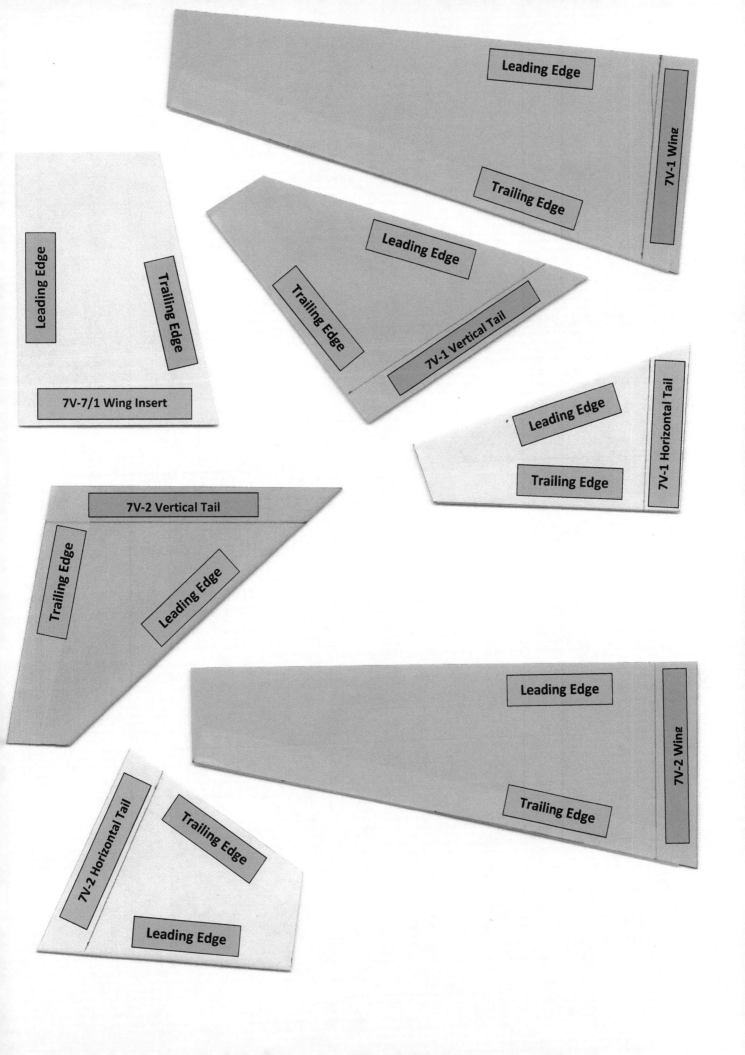

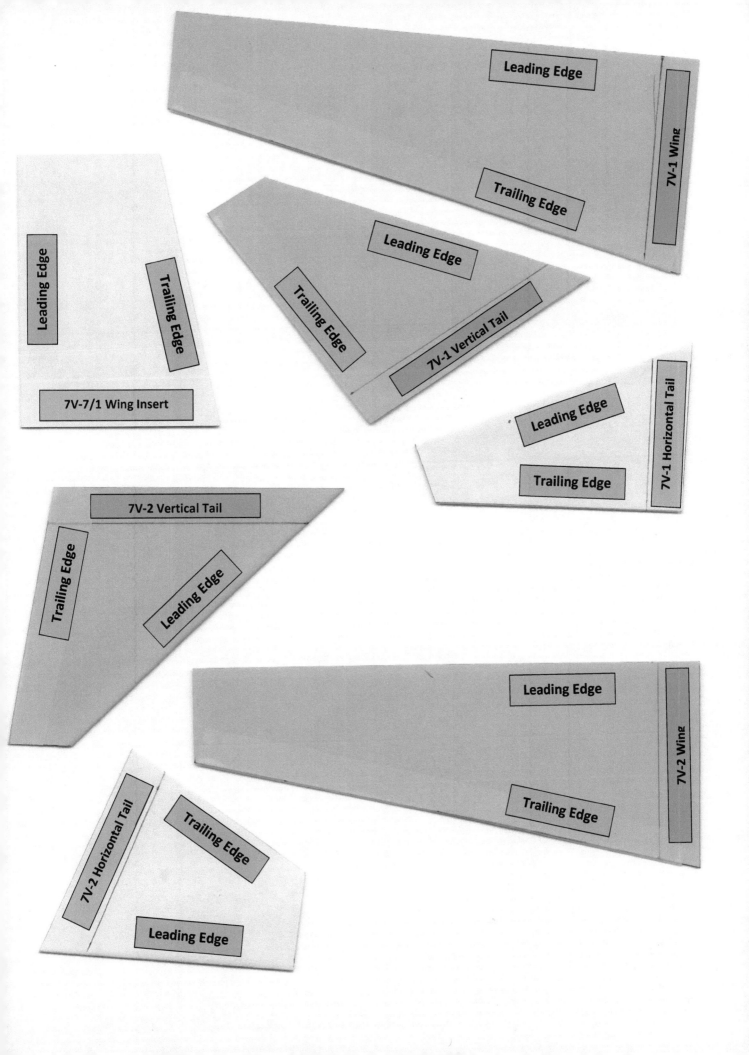

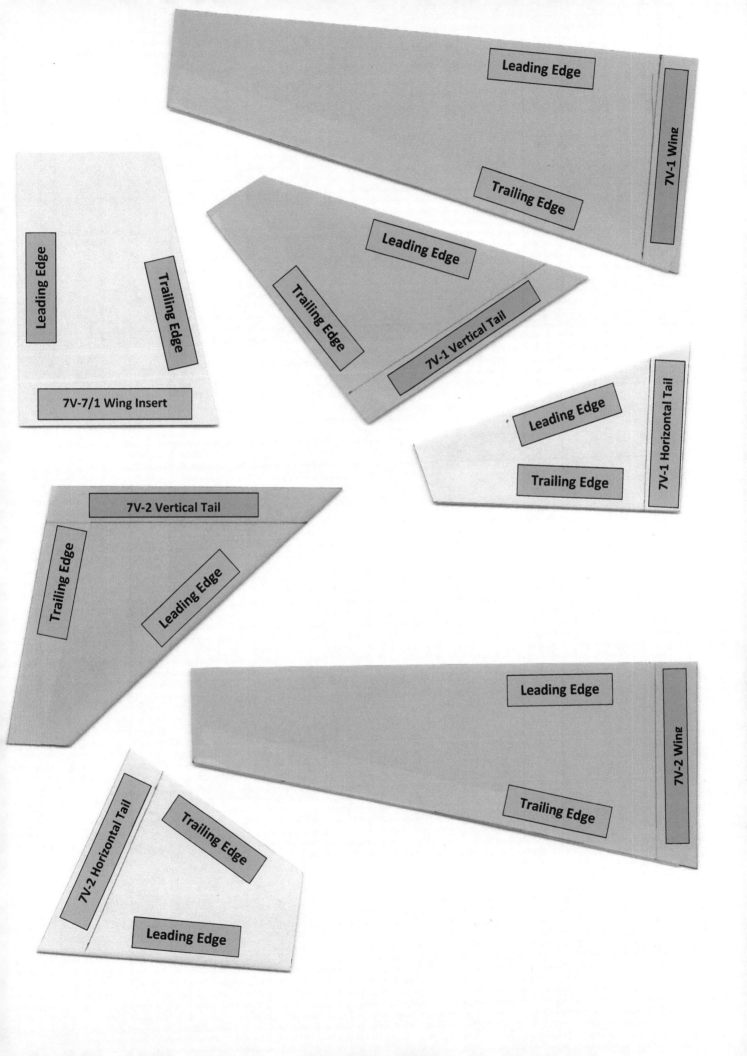

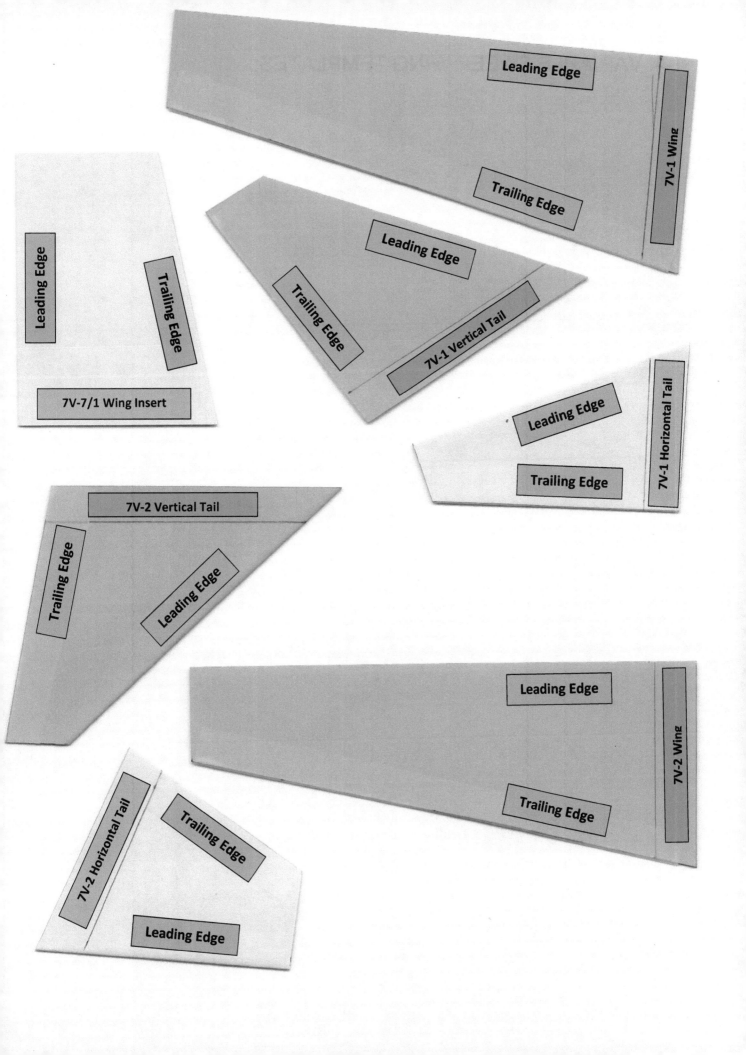

1-4: VARIABLE SWEEP WING TEMPLATES:

8-1 Wing

Leading Edge

Trailing Edge

8-1 Horizontal Tail

Leading Edge

Trailing Edge

Trailing Edge

Leading Edge

8-1 Wing Insert

Trailing Edge

Leading Edge

8-1 Vertical Tail

8-1 Wing

Leading Edge

Trailing Edge

8-1 Horizontal Tail

Leading Edge

Trailing Edge

Trailing Edge

Leading Edge

8-1 Wing Insert

Trailing Edge

Leading Edge

8-1 Vertical Tail

8-1 Wing

Leading Edge

Trailing Edge

8-1 Horizontal Tail

Leading Edge

Trailing Edge

Trailing Edge

Leading Edge

8-1 Wing Insert

Trailing Edge

Leading Edge

8-1 Vertical Tail

8-1 Wing

Leading Edge

Trailing Edge

8-1 Horizontal Tail

Leading Edge

Trailing Edge

Trailing Edge

Leading Edge

8-1 Wing Insert

Trailing Edge

Leading Edge

8-1 Vertical Tail

8-1 Wing

Leading Edge

Trailing Edge

8-1 Horizontal Tail

Leading Edge

Trailing Edge

Trailing Edge

Leading Edge

8-1 Wing Insert

Trailing Edge

Leading Edge

8-1 Vertical Tail

Leading Edge

Trailing Edge

8-2 Wing

Leading Edge

Trailing Edge

8-2 Wing Insert

Trailing Edge

Leading Edge

8-2 Horizontal Tail

Leading Edge

Trailing Edge

8-2 Vertical Tail

Leading Edge

Trailing Edge

8-3 Vertical Tail

Trailing Edge

Leading Edge

8-3 Horizontal Tail

Trailing Edge

Leading Edge

8-3 Wing

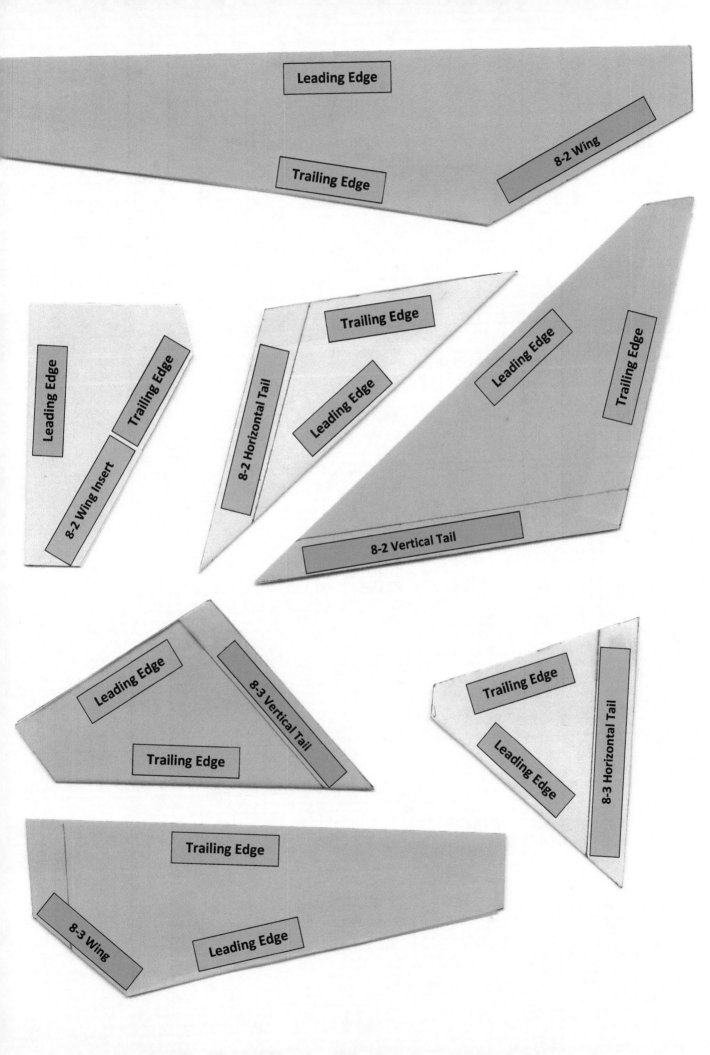

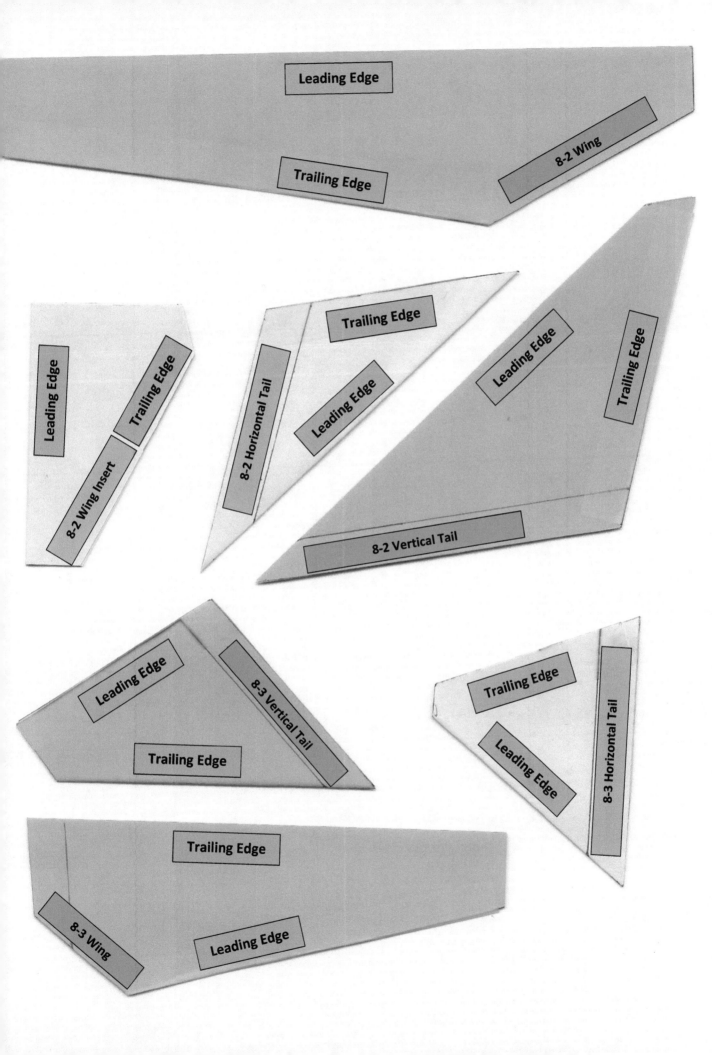

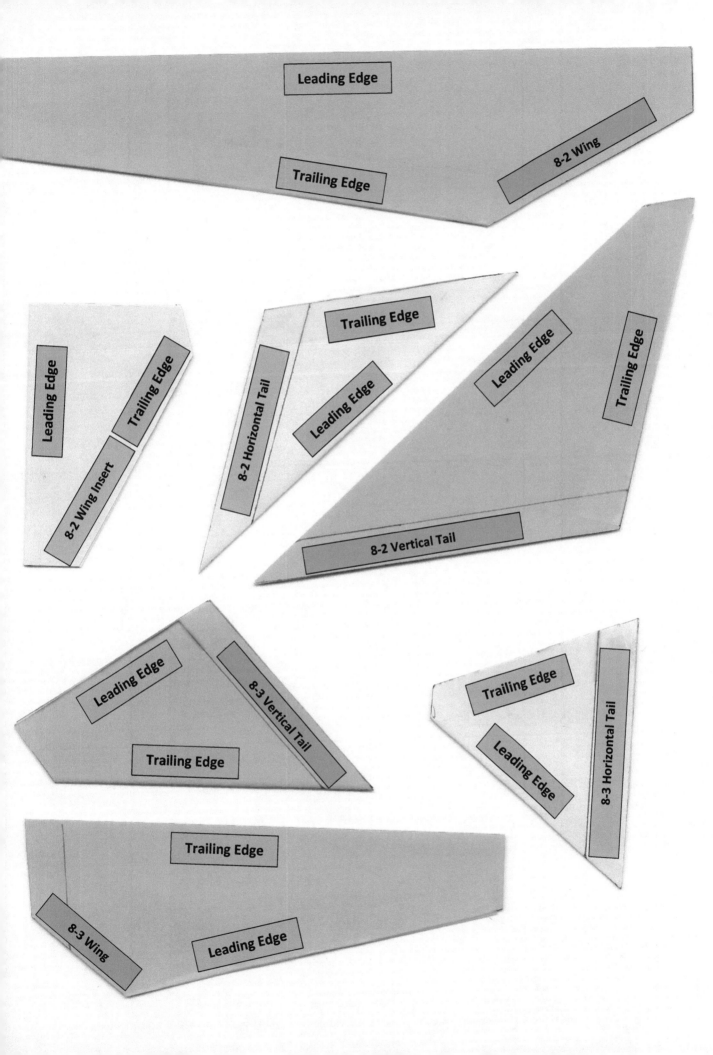

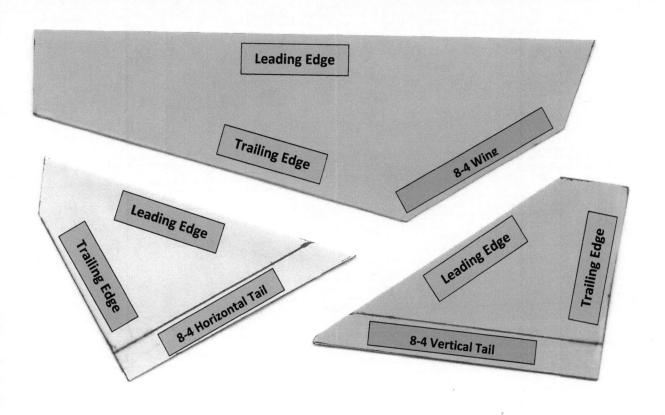

Leading Edge

Trailing Edge

8-4 Wing

Leading Edge

Trailing Edge

8-4 Horizontal Tail

Leading Edge

Trailing Edge

8-4 Vertical Tail

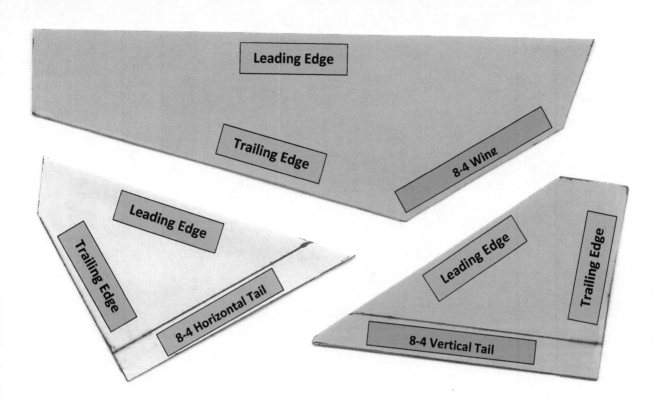

Leading Edge

Trailing Edge

8-4 Wing

Leading Edge

Trailing Edge

8-4 Horizontal Tail

Leading Edge

Trailing Edge

8-4 Vertical Tail

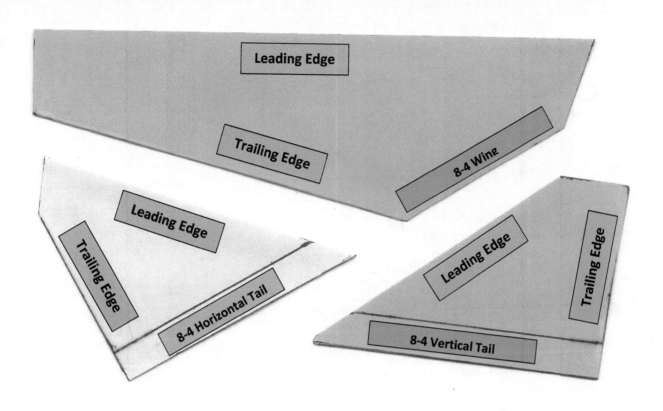

Leading Edge

Trailing Edge

8-4 Wing

Leading Edge

Trailing Edge

8-4 Horizontal Tail

Leading Edge

Trailing Edge

8-4 Vertical Tail

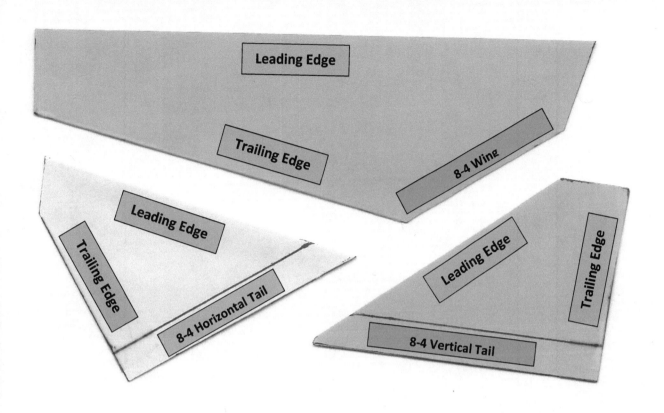

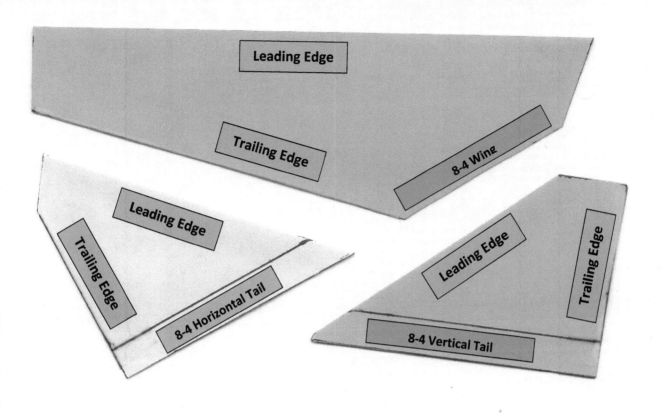

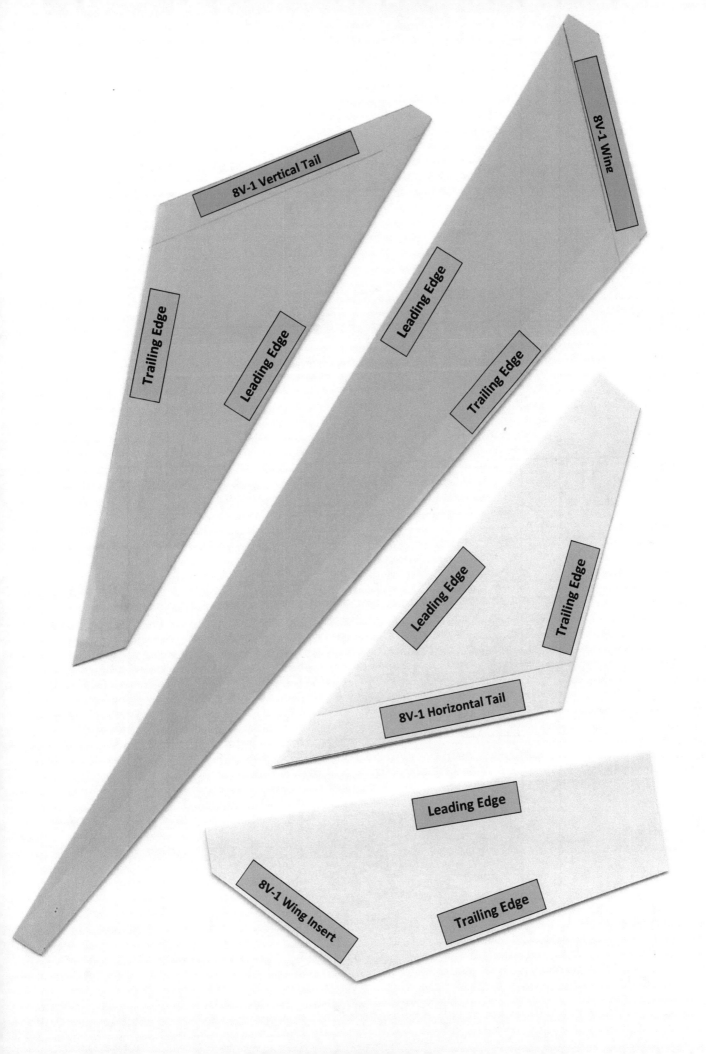

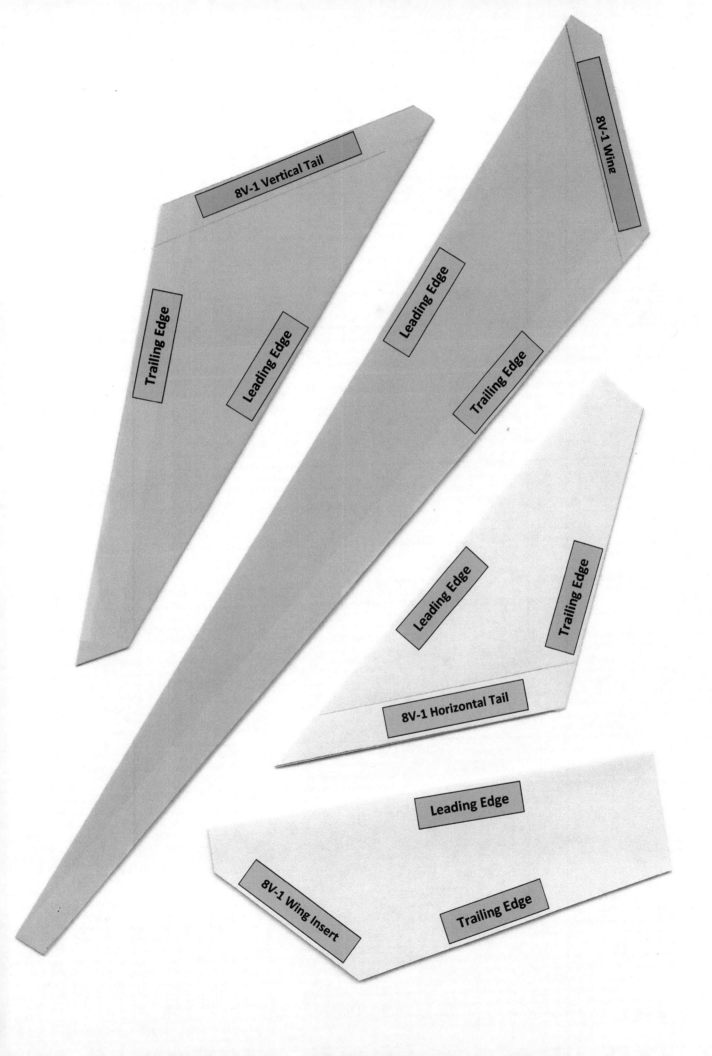

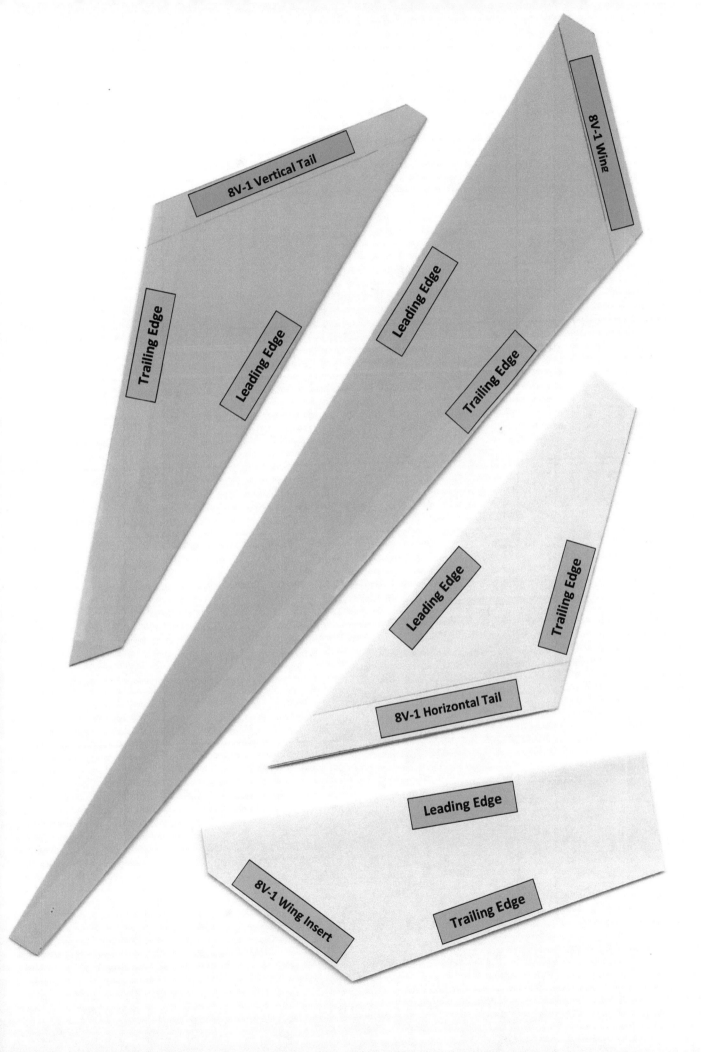

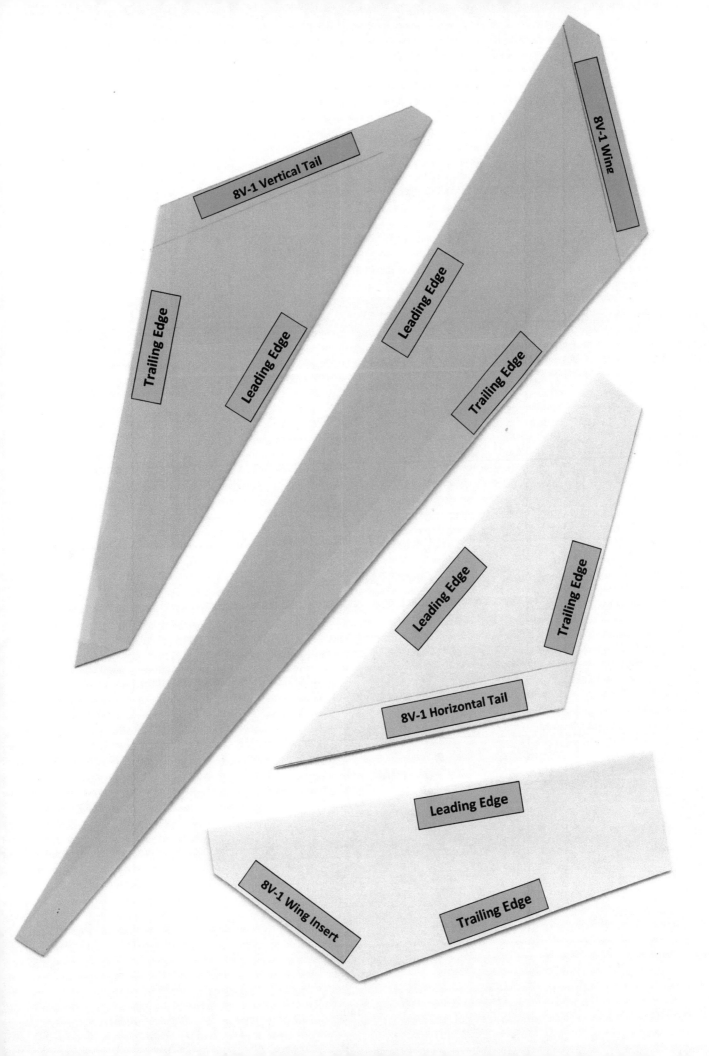

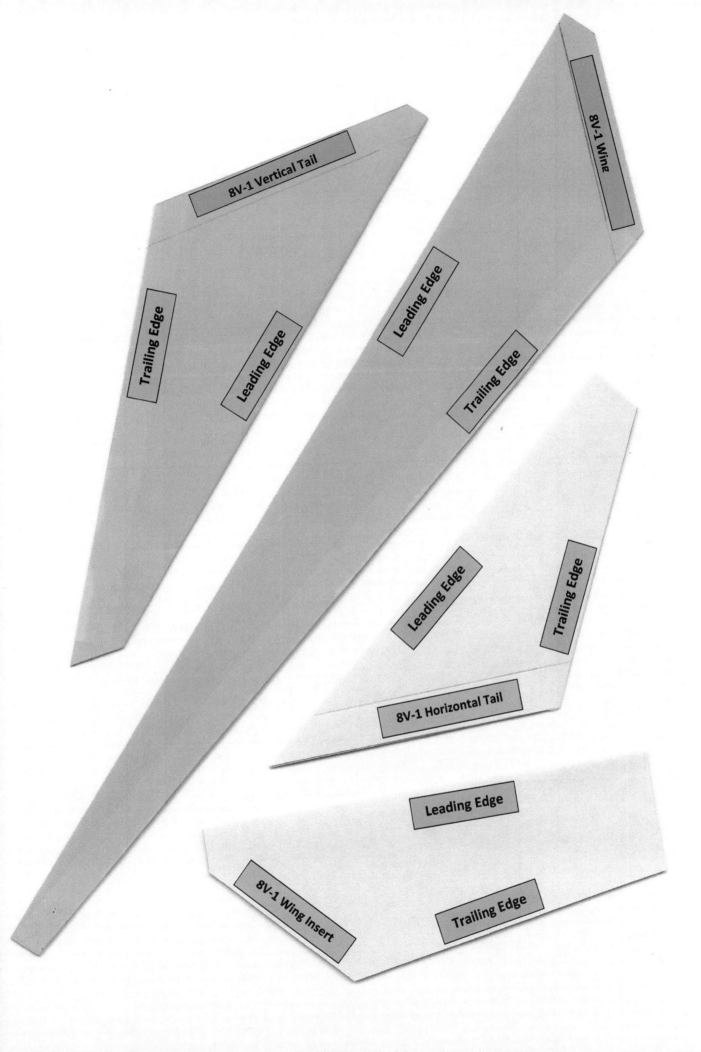

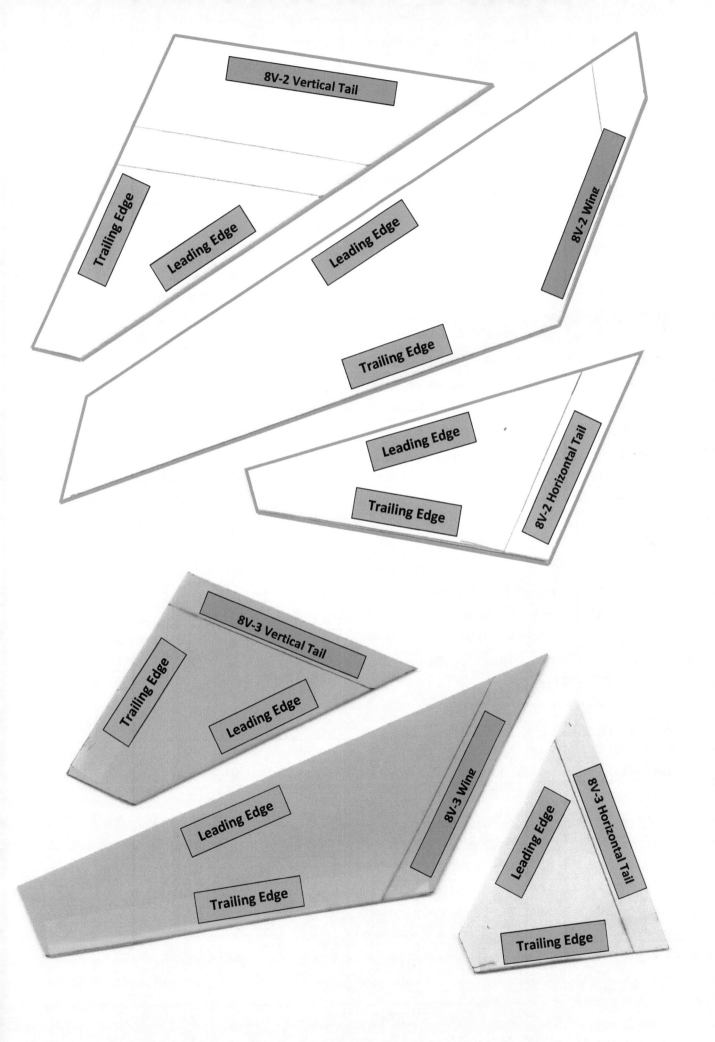

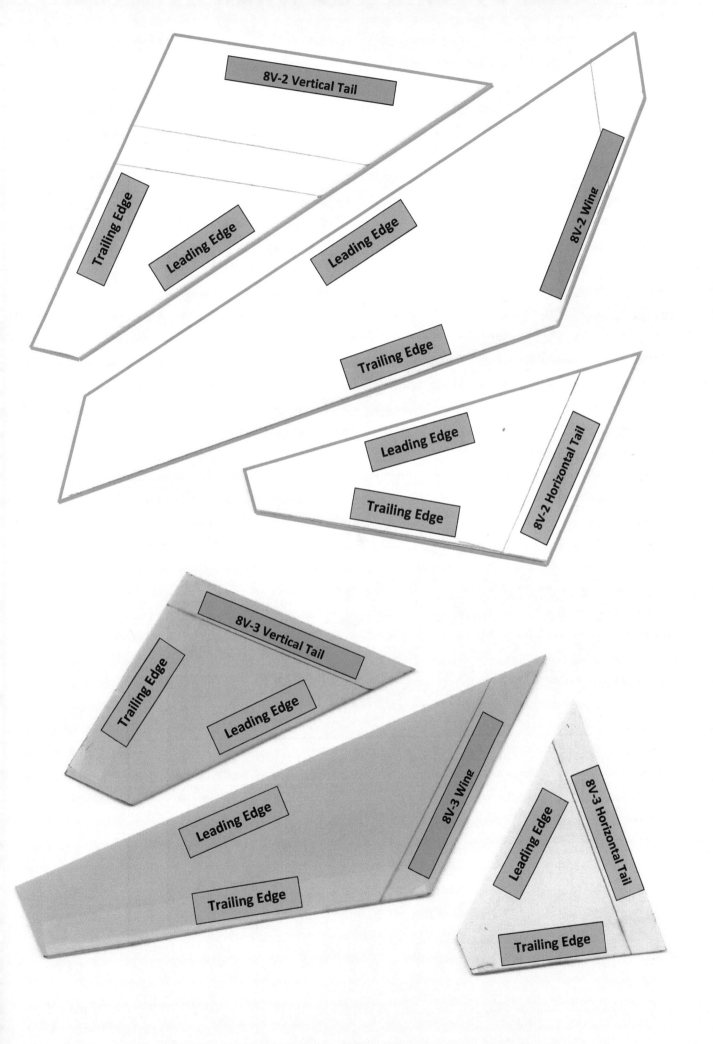

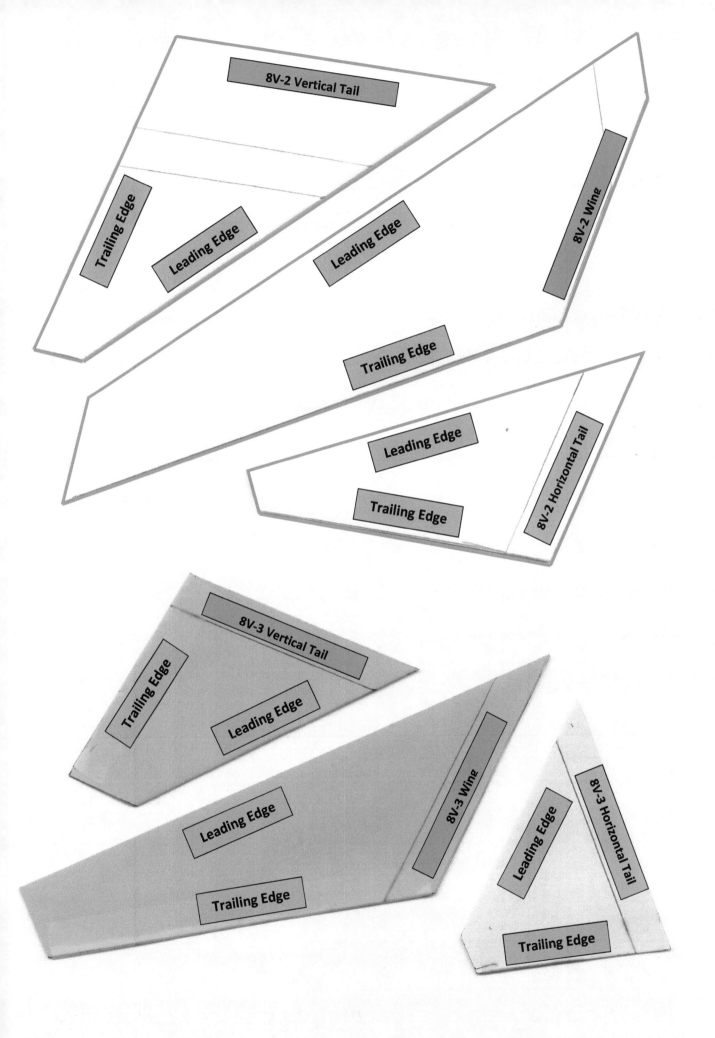

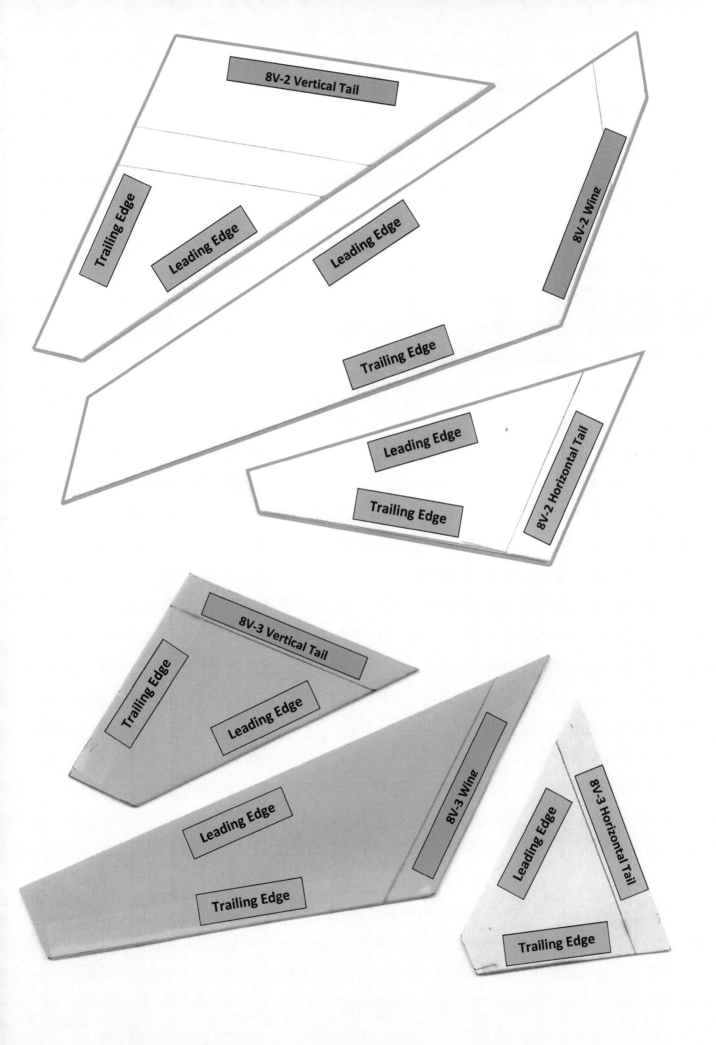

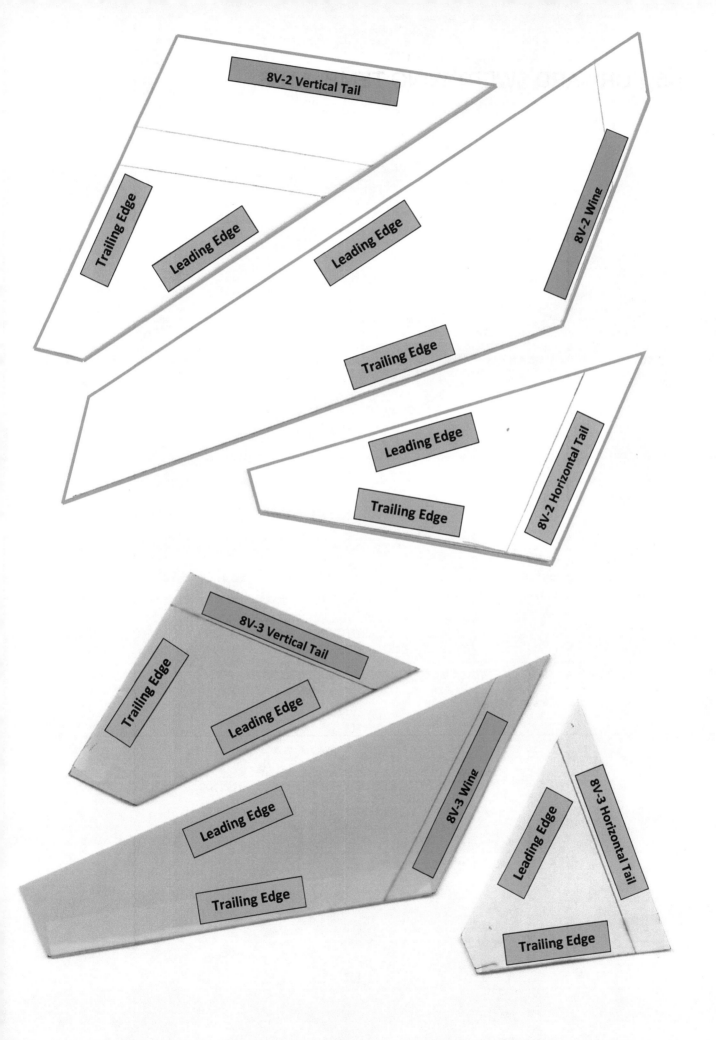

1-5: FORWARD SWEPT WING TEMPLATES:

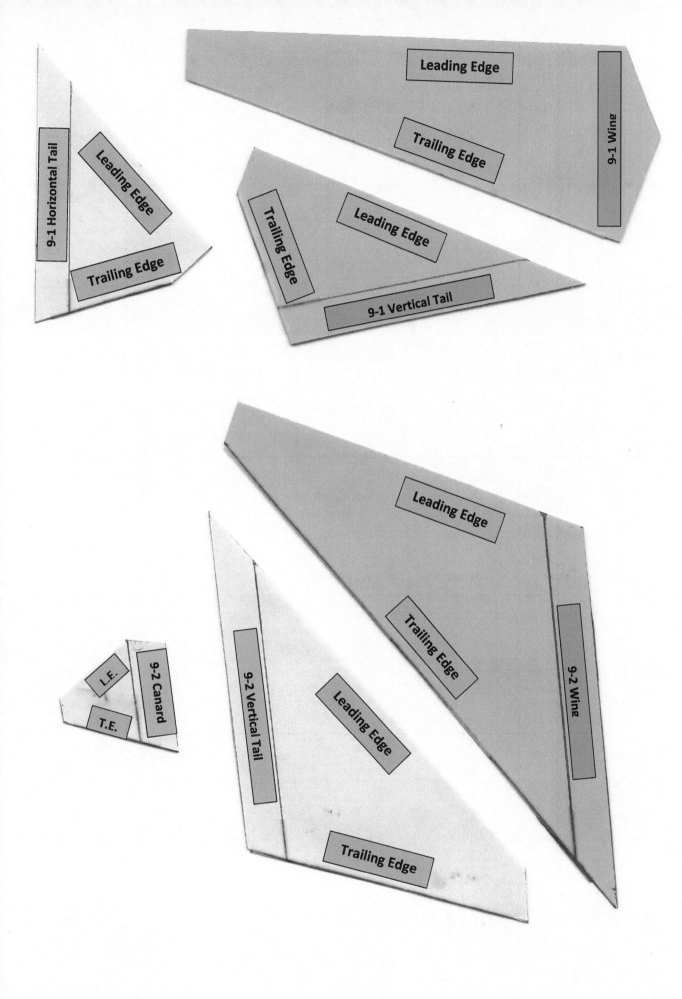

9-1 Horizontal Tail

Leading Edge

Trailing Edge

Leading Edge

Trailing Edge

9-1 Wing

Trailing Edge

Leading Edge

9-1 Vertical Tail

Leading Edge

Trailing Edge

9-2 Wing

L.E.

T.E.

9-2 Canard

9-2 Vertical Tail

Leading Edge

Trailing Edge

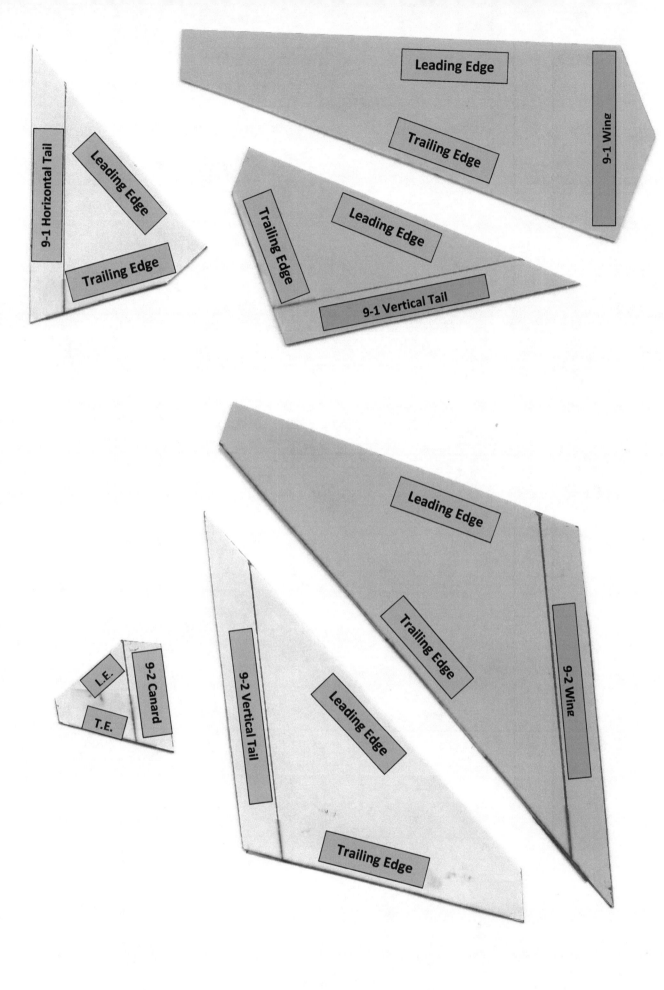

9-1 Horizontal Tail

Leading Edge

Trailing Edge

Leading Edge

Trailing Edge

9-1 Wing

Trailing Edge

Leading Edge

9-1 Vertical Tail

Leading Edge

Trailing Edge

9-2 Wing

L.E.

T.E.

9-2 Canard

9-2 Vertical Tail

Leading Edge

Trailing Edge

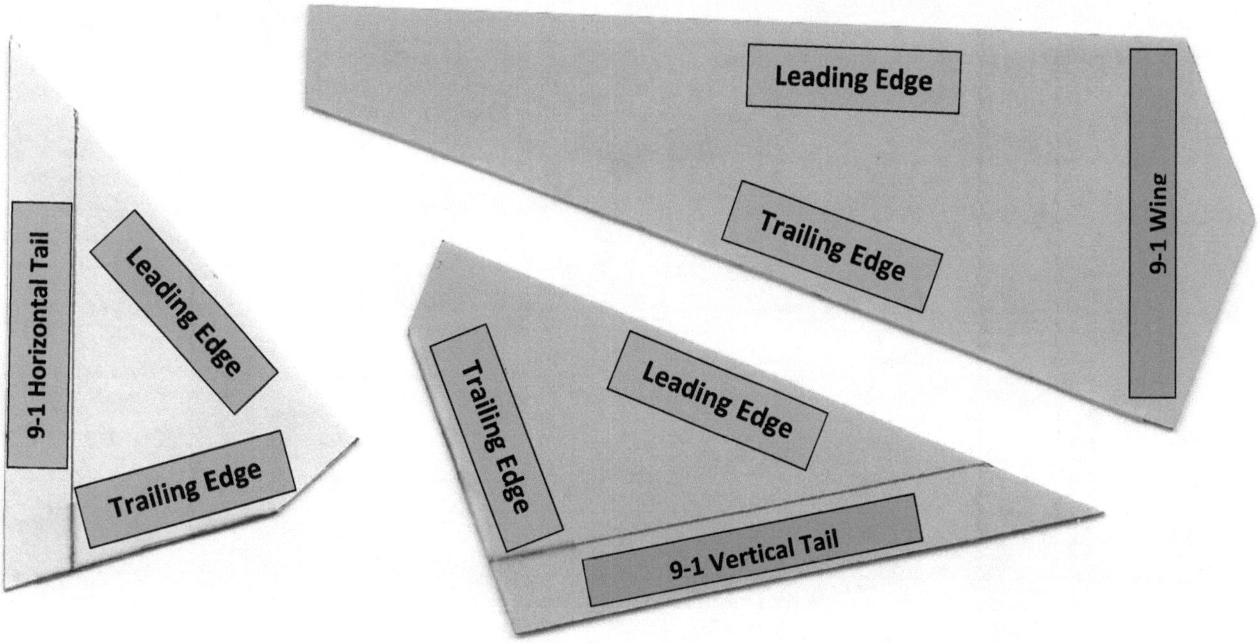
9-1 Horizontal Tail
Leading Edge
Trailing Edge
Leading Edge
Trailing Edge
9-1 Wing
Trailing Edge
Leading Edge
9-1 Vertical Tail

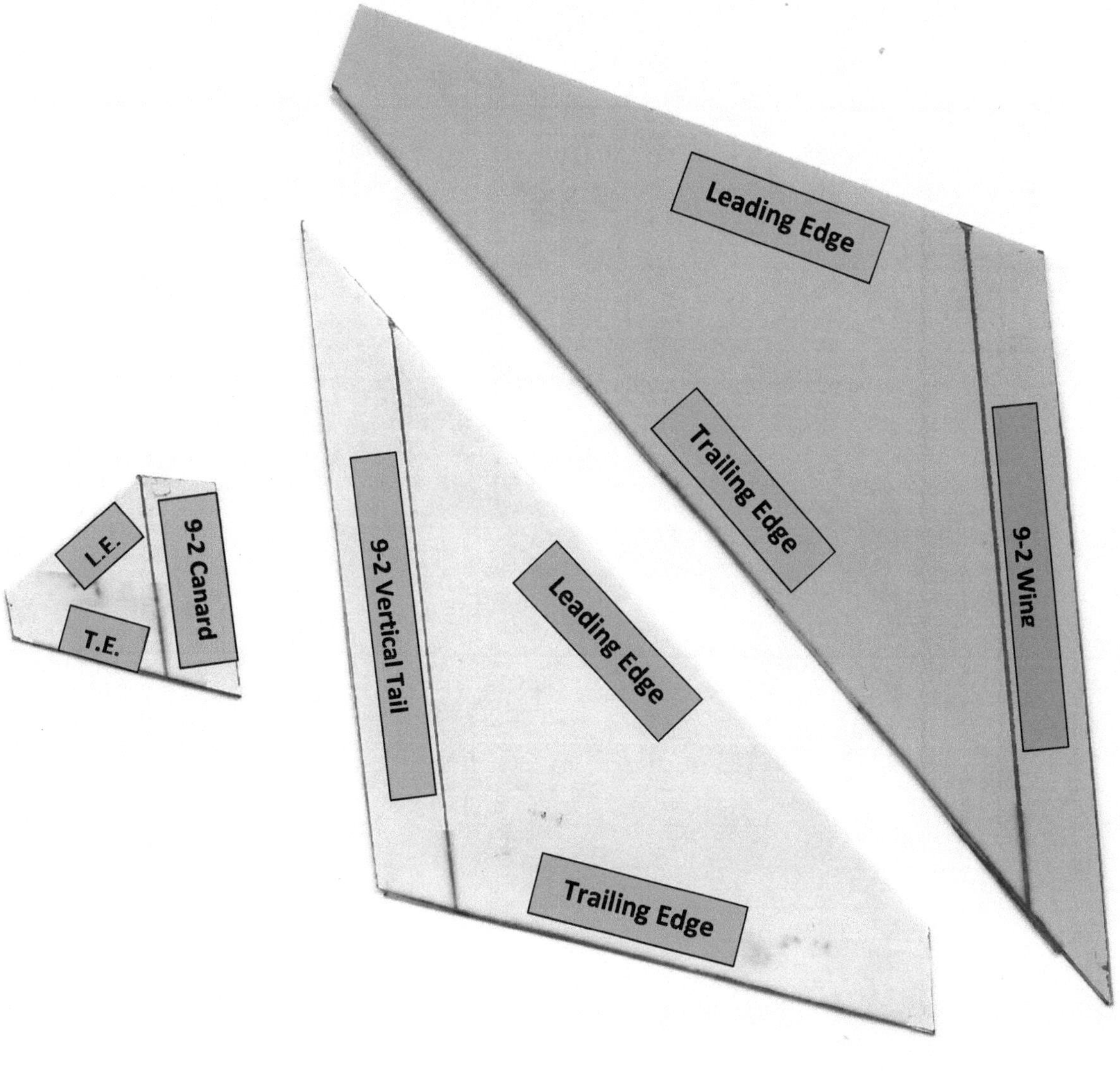
Leading Edge
Trailing Edge
9-2 Wing
9-2 Vertical Tail
Leading Edge
Trailing Edge
L.E.
T.E.
9-2 Canard

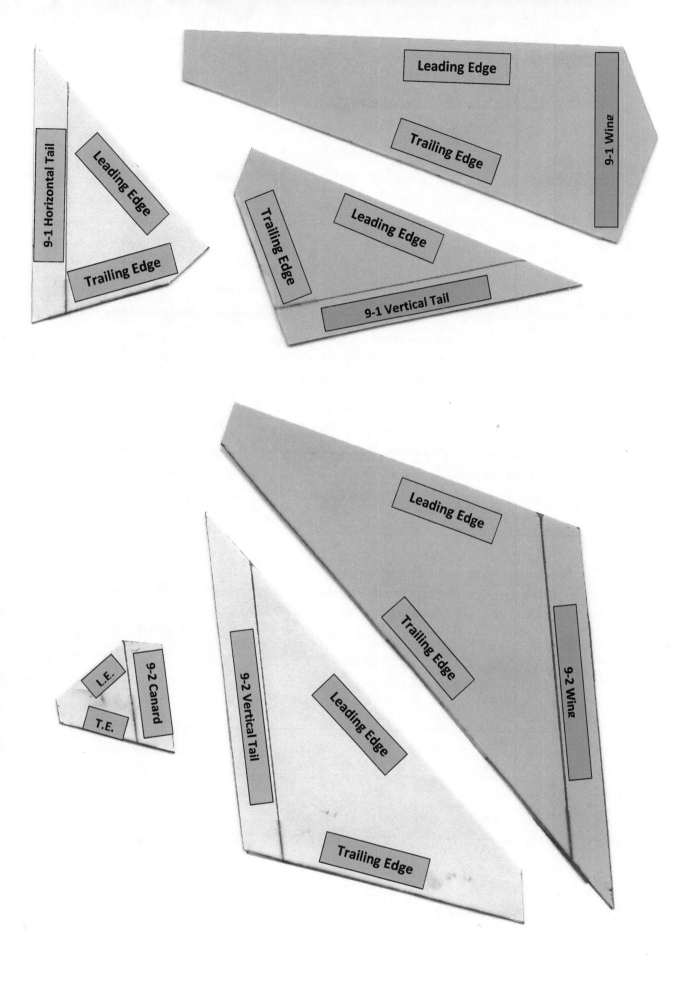

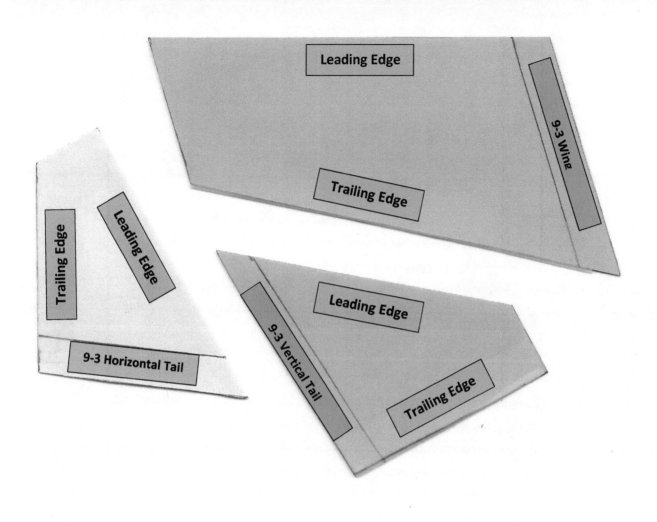

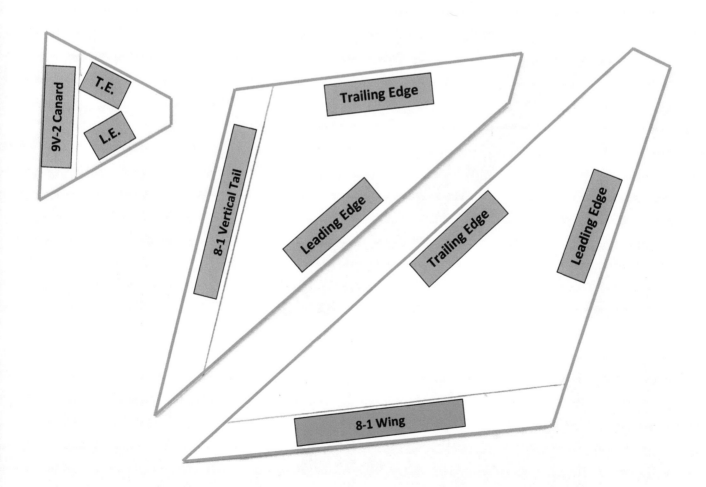

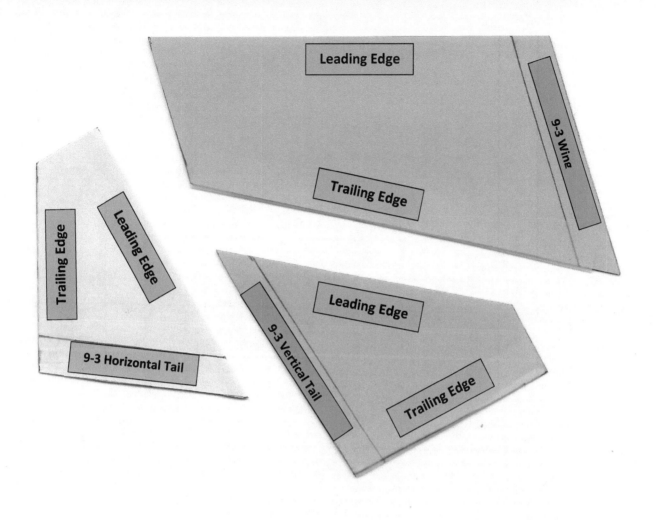

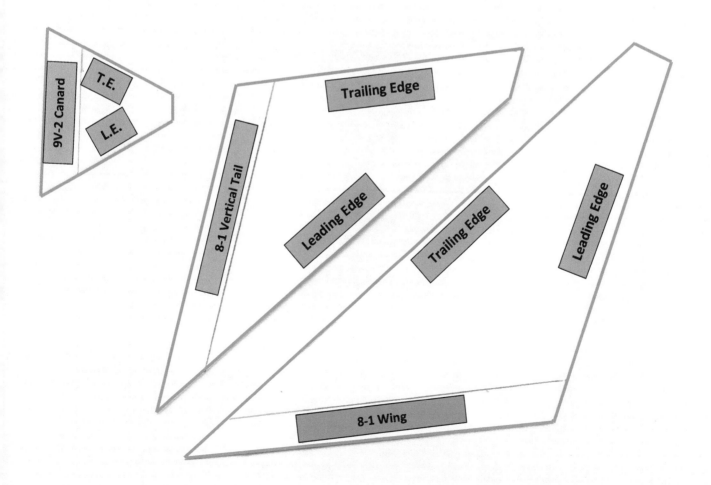

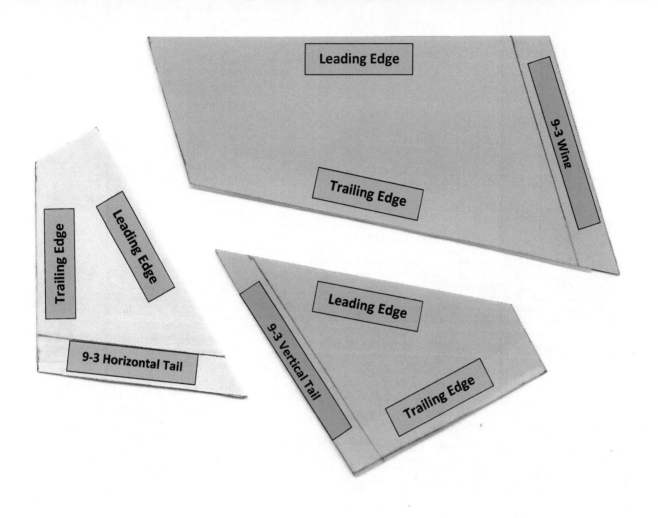

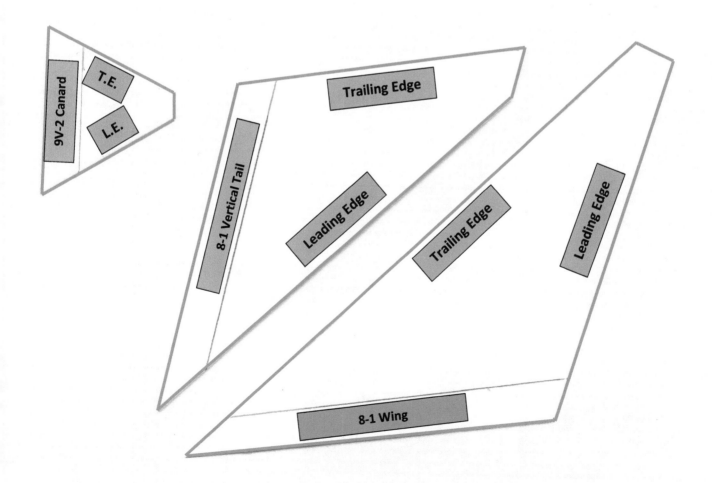

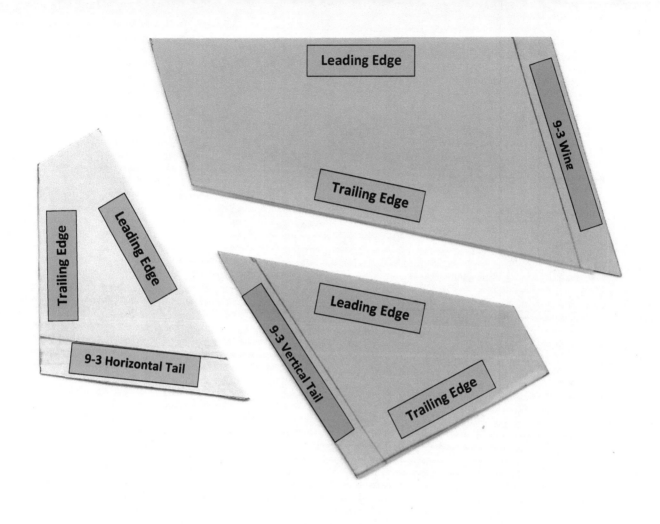

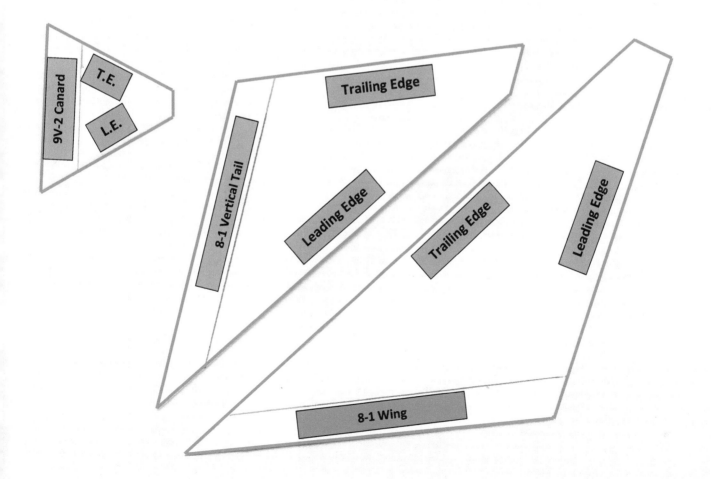

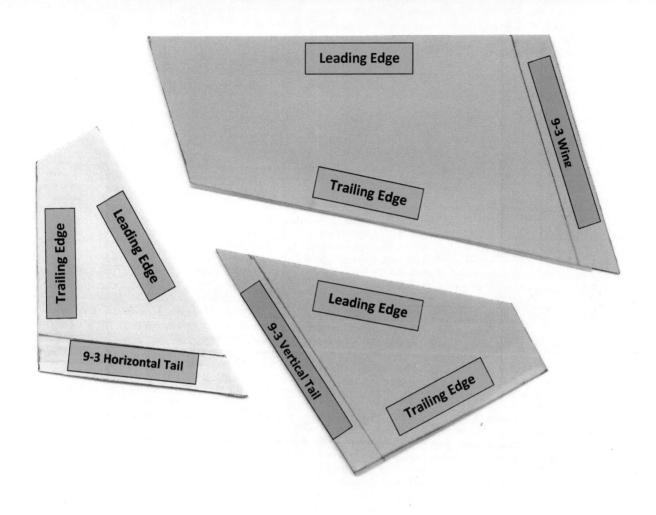

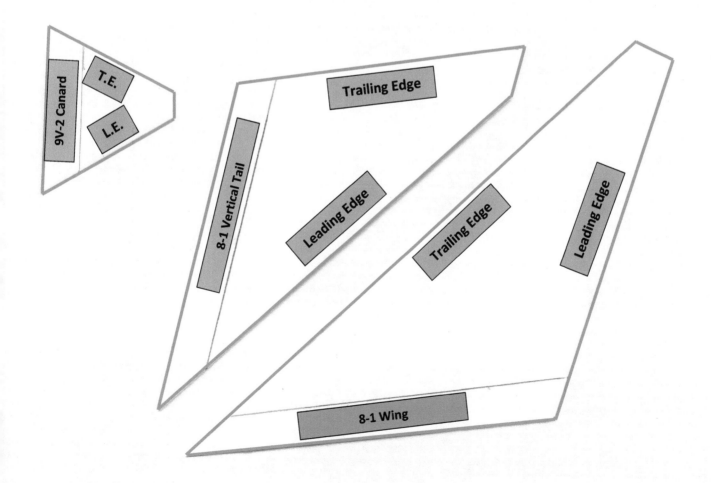

Made in United States
Troutdale, OR
01/09/2024

16817061R00097